The Drovers' Roads
of the Middle Marches

To Naomi, Lucie and Joe … my dearest three

The Drovers' Roads of the Middle Marches

Wayne Smith

Logaston Press

LOGASTON PRESS
Little Logaston Woonton Almeley
Herefordshire HR3 6QH
www.logastonpress.co.uk

First published by Logaston Press May 2013
Copyright © Wayne Smith 2013

Reprinted August 2013

ISBN 978 1 906663 74 2

Typeset by Logaston Press
and printed and bound in Spain by GraphyCemS

Contents

Acknowledgements

To my wife, Naomi Vera-Sanso, for her encouragement and advice, particularly in relation to the choice of photographs, and to Karen and Andy Johnson at Logaston Press for helping shape a whimsy into a reality.

All colour photographs were taken by the author, except those on pages 91 and 117, taken by Lucie Vera-Sanso, and that of the green man on page 80, taken by Richard Hayman. Many thanks to them.

Black and white illustrations in Part One are as follows:

David Cox, 'Keep the Left Road' (page 4), courtesy of Birmingham Museums Trust; 'Archie and Turk' (page 6), from George Lewis's *Henfryn*, Logaston Press; Black Ox Bank sign and bank note (page 11), courtesy of Llandovery Heritage Centre, with special thanks to David Gealy; 'Whitney toll bridge' (page 18), photograph by William Hartland Banks, courtesy of the Ridgebourne Archive; Montgomery drovers (page 20), from the John Thomas collection, by kind permission of Llyfrgell Genedlaethol Cymru / National Library of Wales; Sylvanus Evans (page 28), courtesy of the Museum of Welsh Life, St. Fagans; 'Cilgerran Fair' (page 41), photographed by John Thomas, by kind permission of Llyfrgell Genedlaethol Cymru / National Library of Wales.

And many thanks to Dr Colin Hughes of Builth Wells for revisions to the second printing.

Introduction

The first major portrayal in the English language of Welsh droving, *Wales and the Drovers* (first published in 1943), was written by a Welshman, P.G. Hughes. It is regarded as a seminal work, although his description of the actual routes used is restricted to a few generalised outlines on a large-scale map that simply shows the whole of Wales and the south of England, linking the names of principal towns involved in the trade.

Then, in the 1970s, what became a small herd of volumes on the subject began to appear. In the first year of that decade, K.J. Bonser's *The Drovers* was published, with a specific chapter on 'Drove Roads from the Welsh Border'. The information is slightly more detailed, with a map extending from Shrewsbury down to Bath and across to London, and lines and arrows between places to help the reader to identify what Bonser believed to be the principal routes.

In 1977 Shirley Toulson (with the aid of Fay Godwin's atmospheric photographs) published the first of two books on droving in Wales, *The Drovers' Roads of Wales*. This was the first attempt to provide detailed descriptions of routes, thus enabling readers to set forth in the footsteps of the drover. For Professor R.J. Colyer, whose more academic offering *The Welsh Cattle Drovers* emerged in 1976, Toulson's book was 'a useful work, especially for walkers', but he was concerned that 'many of the roads to which they refer were not connected with the droving trade'. Several routes that he himself proposed, however, particularly in a chapter on droving in his 1984 book *Roads and Trackways of Wales*, appear to marry with those put forward by Toulson.

The aim of this book is two-fold. First, it will pick up the trail of the Welsh drovers as they crossed the border and moved through the central area of the Marches towards the shambles, fairs and markets of England. Most accounts have been largely concerned with drovers' roads within Wales and very little has been written in detail concerning the English side of the trade. One of the main reasons for this has been the gradual eradication of physical evidence in the agricultural lowland areas to the east, which over time have become more enclosed and intensively farmed than the western uplands. My intention is to draw together the topographical details about drovers' roads already outlined elsewhere, and to give evidence for other likely routes that seem not to have been previously identified.

The second aim of the book is to describe the signs and features in a landscape that could indicate a drove way, to help readers discern them for themselves. To this end, I have drawn together received wisdom on the subject, and added some ideas and reflections of my own. Furthermore, I have provided a series of guided walks, incorporating important sections and features of the drovers' roads, which take in some of the most enchanting scenery that this area has to offer. Most of the walks involve varying degrees of incline and decline and all will require the sort of aptitude and apparel that any competent hill walker will be familiar with. The walks are accompanied by sketch-maps, but if you have the Ordnance Survey maps suggested and a smattering of map-reading skills, you should be able to tailor the walks to suit yourself.

I have also included a fictional account of a drove from Tregaron to the Midlands – 'Huw the Drover' – based on historical records and my own imagination. And finally, more detailed facts and figures can be found in the list of books and resources that I have recommended in 'Further Reading'.

The main difficulties of identifying the old drove routes have been a scarcity of archival information detailing specific routes and the gradual eradication over time of physical evidence on the ground and in the field. I have pooled together information from a variety of sources, and added surmises and suggestions of my own. It goes without saying that others will have their own notions and that there will be many localised drove routes still awaiting discovery. I hope that the guidelines for identifying routes will provide insight for the reader and that those who follow the guided walks will enjoy a delightful taste of the great outdoors in this area of central Wales and the middle Marches.

Part One
Drovers and Drovers' Roads
– a brief history

Cue the Drover

The Welsh drovers who walked east out of the hills of Cymru for a thousand years and more made their way with countless generations of cattle, sheep and pigs towards the markets, tables and plates of their more affluent and ever-rapacious English neighbours right up until the end of the nineteenth century. There were still drovers alive and being interviewed after the Second World War who had been involved in the twilight of this ancient art and mystery.

It was the advent of the Industrial Revolution that provided droving with its most demanding times and also sounded its death-knell. With the coming of the railway, drove routes out of Wales were inevitably altered and curtailed. No need now to drive huge herds of animals through the countryside to this or that budding metropolis, when the steam-powered train and cattle wagon could transport all and sundry in a fraction of the time. Drovers had to adapt their routes, and by the middle of the 19th century the main destinations of their trade were the myriad railway stations and cattle sheds that continued to spring up throughout Victorian times in the most remote of Marches towns and Welsh valleys. In the end the age of droving ground to a complete halt, replaced by the age of steam and then by the age of diesel and petrol in the form of the motor engine and the articulated transporter lorry.

That was the end of the droving era. It began long ago; we would have to return some six thousand years into the past to see the very first drovers in these islands. It has been suggested that some of the earliest drove routes date as far back as Neolithic times, when men first started herding animals in Britain, having crossed the ice bridges from their continental and ultimately Middle Eastern and African origins. Pastoralists and herdsmen may have been droving animals for at least a couple of thousand years before they found their way to these shores. The earliest drove ways were invariably to be found (alongside the earliest settlements) on higher ground and especially along the natural ridgeways – those

Herefordshire artist David Cox's watercolour 'Keep the Left Road'

long stretches of upland that connected one area of lowland with another. One of the most renowned of these in the Marches area is the Kerry Ridgeway, which ranges east, just south of Newtown, all the way to Bishop's Castle.

Originally drove ways would have been created by the movement of livestock from one place to another within a certain locality – say between villages and farms within the same area, or between different pastures within the same farm: for example between the lowland, winter dwelling (known as the *hendre* in Wales) and the upland, summer one (the *hafod*). This seasonal movement of humans and their livestock is known as 'transhumance', and could be said to differ from what we term droving in that the latter is a term associated primarily with the movement of animals for sale.

In time, with the rise in importance of fairs and markets during the medieval period, drove roads would stretch between different counties, as farmers sought out market towns and regional fairs to sell their livestock. Part of the art of droving lay in determining the length of time each journey should take: move too slowly and market day would be missed, but travel too fast and animals could arrive out of condition, even lame. With the expansion of urban settlements during the Industrial Revolution, animals were taken even further afield from their Celtic homelands, towards the growing conurbations of England. Many ended up in the 'fattening fields' of the Midlands, particularly in the counties of Warwickshire, Leicestershire and Northamptonshire, where animals were sold to farmers who would fatten them up in the better pastures to be found there, before selling them on to other farmers or to the slaughterhouse. The land and climate of Wales was not conducive to the growing of sufficient pasture, the storage of fodder over winter months, or the production of the cereal crops required for the rearing and keeping of good quality beef cattle. Most families in the Welsh uplands would have had just enough land, cereal and fodder to support themselves and maybe a solitary pig during the harsh winter months,

> **A Royal Connection**
> Prior to the Battle of Bosworth Field in 1485, Henry Tudor was joined near Welshpool by two Welsh supporters, William ap Griffiths of Penrhyn and Richard ap Howell of Mostyn, who were each accompanied by such herds of Welsh Black cattle that Henry's ever-expanding army was able to march on to victory.

This account of a drove arriving at the Barnet Fair – which took place on the 18th and 19th of October each year – appeared in an edition of the *Farmer's Magazine* in 1856. Any discernible bias is no doubt the result of its being written by an Englishman:

Imagine some hundreds of bullocks like an immense forest of horns, propelled hurriedly towards you amid the hideous and uproarious shouting of a set of semi-barbarous drovers who value a restive bullock far beyond the life of a human being, driving their mad and noisy herds over every person they meet if not fortunate enough to get out of their way; closely followed by a drove of unbroken wild Welsh ponies, fresh from their native hills, all of them loose and unrestrained as the oxen that preceded them; kicking, rearing and biting each other amid the unintelligible anathemas of their human attendants ... the noisy 'hurrahs' of lots of 'un-English speaking' Welshmen who may have just sold some of their native bovine stock whilst they are to be seen throwing up their long-worn, shapeless hats high in the air, as a type of Taffy's delight, uttering at the same time a trade [sic] of gibberish which no-one can understand but themselves.

According to George Lewis (in his book *Henfryn*) Archie once played football for Arsenal, but he later became a drover, based near Abbeycwmhir, and he is pictured here with his dog Turk.

let alone feeding any number of cattle and sheep. Hence the handing over of animals to the drovers, who would move from farm to farm and fair to fair taking charge of beasts, generally without payment, on the understanding that recompense would be made on their return from England. When enough animals were assembled they would gather at one of several main collecting points situated throughout Wales before heading east.

The average drove consisted of 300 cattle between 3 and 4 years of age, plus some milk ('milch') cows and a few bulls. The average speed – about 2 miles per hour and covering between 15 to 20 miles per day – would allow the animals to graze at the wayside, while being steady enough to prevent them from becoming over-stretched and out of condition. Even at this steady pace they would lose a considerable percentage of their body-weight in the course of a journey, and some wealthier drovers went to the length of purchasing pasture-land in the Midlands where their charges could be restored to a full, blooming health before they went to market.

The majority of sales would be between April and June, especially if the beasts were sold to the Midlands farmers who would fatten them up on their summer grass. Another peak time was during the autumn, when farmers needed beasts for de-pasturing:

Veterinary practice on the hoof

It was not uncommon for drovers to have to treat their animals for a variety of ailments and afflictions. Some of their notebooks have survived, containing a wide range of 'recipes' meant to do the trick, some of which would appear completely extraordinary to the modern eye. For example Gervase Markhan in his book of 1623, *Husbandry of Beastes*, recommends the following as a cure-all for 'pestilence, garygll or murrain':

'Give to all your Cattell, as well the sound as the sicke, the medicine, which never failed to preserve as many as have taken it: Take of old strong urine a quart, and mix it with more than half a handful of hens dung well dissolved therein, and give it to your beast to drink.'

By the 18th century murrain (foot-and-mouth) was commonly dealt with by the large-scale fumigation of cattle using smoke. Sometimes the fires were so large as to obscure large herds and could be seen from miles around. Even rough and ready surgery was called upon at times. For example, mastitis was treated simply by the sliced removal of the teat with a sharpened knife.

that is, grazing bare fields prior to the winter frosts. Down through the centuries, though, the greatest draw for most drovers would have been the markets further south offered by the dealers and butchers of London and the Home Counties, not forgetting the insatiable demand of His or Her Majesty's Army and Navy, who needed meat to march on and sail by, to support them in a seemingly endless succession of wars and campaigns.

The Sabbath
From the time of the Reformation a variety of laws and by-laws were originated regarding the Sabbath, many of which affected the drovers and their droving trade. For example:

> Noe Drover, Horsecourser, Waggoner, Butcher, Higler, or any of their servants shall travell or come into ... an Inne or lodgeing upon the Lord's Day or any part thereof ... upon pain that each and every such offender shall forfeit twenty shillings for every such offence.

A disregard for this law was probably the reason why two drovers from Wales found themselves in a Herefordshire court being prosecuted for 'profanation of the Sabbath in driving cattle through the village of Mordiford in Herefordshire'. The court hoped that 'such legal interference will tend to check a practice which has of late been too general and must have proved truly painful to the Christian observer'.

In the capital city drovers were subject to even more decrees restricting and regulating their business. For example, it was forbidden to drive cattle towards Smithfield before midnight on Sundays, or within one mile of it on market days, an attempt to force drovers to drive animals through the streets when traffic was at its lowest. Convictions could also be handed out for drovers found to be drunk in charge of their beasts. Recorded sentences ranged from fines of forty shillings to imprisonment for one month. A Welshman, Humphrey ap Phillip, prosecuted for being drunk and using obscene language, received a sentence of five days in 1875. Another man, George Mussin, had to pay a five shilling fine 'for being drunk and incapable of taking care of himself in Offord Road, Islington'.

Smithfield Market

En route to a robbery, Bill Sikes leads Oliver Twist through Smithfield Market, the endpoint for many a Welsh animal. Here Dickens brings the scene to life:

Turning down Sun Street and Crown Street, and crossing Finsbury Square, Mr. Sikes struck, by way of Chiswell Street, into Barbican: thence into Long Lane, and so into Smithfield; from which latter place arose a tumult of discordant sounds that filled Oliver Twist with amazement.

It was market-morning. The ground was covered, nearly ankle-deep, with filth and mire; a thick steam, perpetually rising from the reeking bodies of the cattle, and mingling with the fog, which seemed to rest upon the chimney-tops, hung heavily above. All the pens in the centre of the large area, and as many temporary pens as could be crowded into the vacant space, were filled with sheep; tied up to posts by the gutter side were long lines of beasts and oxen, three or four deep. Countrymen, butchers, drovers, hawkers, boys, thieves, idlers, and vagabonds of every low grade, were mingled together in a mass; the whistling of drovers, the barking of dogs, the bellowing and plunging of oxen, the bleating of sheep, the grunting and squeaking of pigs, the cries of hawkers, the shouts, oaths, and quarrelling on all sides; the ringing of bells and roar of voices, that issued from every public-house; the crowding, pushing, driving, beating, whooping, and yelling; the hideous and discordant din that resounded from every corner of the market; and the unwashed, unshaven, squalid, and dirty figures constantly running to and fro, and bursting in and out of the throng; rendered it a stunning and bewildering scene, which quite confounded the senses.

Mr. Sikes, dragging Oliver after him, elbowed his way through the thickest of the crowd, and bestowed very little attention on the numerous sights and sounds, which so astonished the boy. He nodded, twice or thrice, to a passing friend; and, resisting as many invitations to take a morning dram, pressed steadily onward, until they were clear of the turmoil, and had made their way through Hosier Lane into Holborn.

Animal rights

Other ordinances approved in London were intended to regulate the way drovers treated their charges. For example, drovers were prohibited from using 'any stick or other instrument the point of which shall be of greater length than one quarter of an inch'. Anyone contravening this regulation could be subject to a fine of up to forty shillings. In 1875 a drover, Edward Cook, was fined twenty-four shillings 'for cruelly beating a calf in York Road'. An even harsher sentence was meted out to a James Bailey 'for cruelly torturing a cow' – he received fourteen days hard labour.

Drovers as financiers

The economic contribution that the Welsh drovers made to their nation's wealth, even to the extent of playing an important role in the foundation and development of its banking systems, has been well documented. Contradicting the received opinion of many that the droving fraternity consisted of knaves and ne'er-do-wells, drovers were regularly dealing with financial transactions involving large amounts of money, as well as being asked to carry mail, goods and money not connected with the droving trade on behalf of others, including rents owed to landlords in the City by tenants on their estates in Wales and amounts of money being sent to relatives who lived in England.

For example, as far back as 1624, Henry, the son of Sir John Wynn of Gwydir Castle in the Conwy valley, wrote a letter of complaint to his father regarding the small amount sent to him in the safe-keeping of a drover, one David Lloyd. It seems that 'old David Lloyd, the drover' was still involved in the Wynn family business some 37 years later, for in 1661 he was in possession of a bill that was to be exchanged for the sum of £65, a transaction handled by a Henry Maurice who resided at the King's Head in Fleet Street. And in 1734 the squire of Henblas on Anglesey, Thomas Bulkeley, requested in a letter that a drover, one Thomas Lewis, pay his son, who was working in London as a clerk at the time, the sum of £15. Drovers also worked on behalf of the Crown. For example, it is recorded that in 1636, during the reign of Charles I, Welsh drovers were called upon to play the role of government agents, in that they were given the responsibility of transporting 'Ship Money' from port officials on the Welsh coast down to London.

To avoid the danger of carrying large quantities of cash and being waylaid by highwaymen, the sums involved were more often than not deducted from the sales of animals made in the capital. Such ways of dealing with finances eventually led to the establishment of the first bank in Wales. Thus was born in 1799 at the King's Head Inn, Llandovery, Carmarthenshire, the Black Ox Bank, set up by a Welsh drover who went by the name of David Jones. The Banc yr Eidion Ddu issued banknotes that bore the engraving of a black ox and, being only issued and received by those the bank knew to be of good repute, they proved worthless to villains. Following the appointment of agents in London, branches were eventually opened that could deal in these notes, and in 1909 the Black Ox was assimilated by Lloyds Bank. A similar bank, Banc yr Ddafad Ddu, primarily for sheep dealers, was set up in Aberystwyth; its notes bore black sheep (£1) and lambs (10 shillings), the number of animals depicted signifying the value of the note.

Literary drovers
Equally important has been the part drovers played in the social and cultural growth of Wales down through the ages. Many drovers, after they

The sign of the Black Ox Bank and (above) one of its banknotes

had retired to a more settled way of life, seem to have become important figures in their communities. Some turned their hand to schoolteaching and preaching, while several became pre-eminent literary figures of their day. This is perhaps not surprising when you consider that head drovers had to be fluent in a foreign language (English), have a good grasp of mathematics and business, and be articulate and confident enough to deal with the great variety of types and social standings of people they met in the course of their droving. Also, spending your life striding through some of the most picturesque countryside and panoramic vistas that Britain had to offer must have had an effect on the psyche, especially when the vast majority of the population would never have ventured further afield than the next valley or nearest town.

'Advice to the Dealer or Drover'
From the Welsh poet Rees Pritchard (1579 – 1644):

If thou'rt a Dealer, honest be each act,
And fairly pay for what to thee is sold;
Be to thy promise and thy word exact:
Credit is better oft than hoards of gold.

Of the necessitous no vantage take,
And be not studious of excessive gain,
With rogues no bargain or agreement make;
Nothing will thrive that comes from such a train.

Buy not too much on tick, for all will sell,
To such a purchaser, extremely dear,
And such a trade will soon that wretch compel
To quit the kingdom, or to disappear.

Take heed that thou dost not thy chapmen cheat,
God will a sentence pass on all deceit:

And tho' thou shou'dst beyond the seas retreat,
Sure vengeance will on thy transgression wait.

They ne'er (the scripture on that head is plain)
Shall roast the prey, who study to deceive:
For fraud to no one yet brought real gain,
It passes off, like water through a sieve.

Of drunkenness beware, whate'er thou dost;
For drunkenness will make the wealthiest poor,
And when a trader's oft in liquor lost,
In wine and ale he soon will spend his store.

Take care of thy dear soul, to justice cleave,
And do the poor no wrong, for conscience' sake:
For if a bankrupt thou the land shou'dst leave,
Vengeance divine thy footsteps will o'ertake.

Perhaps the most famous of literary drovers was Dafydd Jones of Caeo (1711-77), who not only translated hymns into Welsh but wrote several famous ones that are still sung to this day. His dramatic conversion to Christianity is sometimes even compared to that of St. Paul. It so happened that one Sabbath day, as he returned home from a drove, Dafydd found himself transfixed by the dulcet sound of the hymns being sung within the chapel of Troedrhiwdalar. Unable to resist, he ventured inside, an impulse that became a turning point in his life. From that day on he was devoutly committed to the faith and transformed into the renowned hymnologist still celebrated today. Edward Morus of Perthi Llwydion, who is considered one of the greatest Welsh poets of the seventeenth century, was also highly regarded by those with whom he did droving business, and considered to have an unimpeachable character. Another whose reputation was held in the highest regard was Benjamin Evans of Pembrokeshire who, in 1769, became pastor of Yr Hen chapel in Llanuwchlyn.

Many drovers helped to support various publications and journals. One example, *Wales' Golden Treasury,* had as subscribers, along with the likes of Dr. Samuel Johnson, Hugh Jones of Bala, drover, Thomas Roberts of Llwyn Cwm, drover, Thomas Jones of Ty Isaf, drover, Hugh Parry, Penmorfa, drover, and John Thomas of Bala, drover.

The Welsh Black

The Welsh Black was the predominant cattle breed dealt with by the Welsh drovers. It is similar in size and colour to the extinct ancestor of all European cattle, the Auroch, and has been linked to breeds found in the Iberian peninsula and the south of France. In the past, animals of a more speckled and

At swim two cows ...

The Isle of Anglesey was renowned as the producer of fine Welsh Blacks and by 1810 it is estimated that some 14,000 cattle were being exported to the markets of the Midlands from here and the pastures of the Lleyn peninsula. This poem, by Richard Llwyd, describes their crossing of the treacherous Menai Straits:

> These are the features of the ferrying fair,
> And those that dote on discord may go there
> The tides, contending with the toiling boats,
> The horny forest that on Menai floats
> The brutes inferior, but by the windy storm,
> The living beach where bellowing droves depart,
> And the last low, that rends the suffering heart.

13

It fortunately happened that several herds of black cattle that had been reared in Anglesey, were then crossing the Menai Strait, on their road to Abergeley fair, where they are bought up by drovers, and disposed of at Barnet fair to the farmers in the neighbourhood, who fatten them for the London market. We were much amused with seeing a large herd driven over. They are urged in a body by loud shoutings and blows into the water, and as they swim well and fast, usually make their way for the opposite shore. The whole troop proceeds pretty regularly till it arrives within about a hundred and fifty yards of the landing place, when, meeting with a rapid current formed by the tide, eddying, and rushing with great violence between the rocks that encroach far into the channel, the herd is thrown into the utmost confusion. Some of the boldest and strongest push directly across, and presently reach the land. The more timorous immediately turn round, and endeavour to gain the place from which they set off; but the greater part, borne down by the force of the stream, are carried towards Beaumaris Bay, and frequently float to a great distance before they are able to reach the Caernarvonshire shore. To prevent accidents, a number of boats well manned, attend, who row after the stragglers to force them to join the main body; and if they are very obstinate, the boatmen throw ropes about their horns, and fairly tow them to the shore, which resounds with loud bellowing of those that are landed, and are shaking their wet sides. Notwithstanding the great number of cattle that annually pass the strait, an instance seldom, if ever, occurs of any being lost, though they are frequently carried to the very entrance of the Menai in Beaumaris Bay.

From Arthur Aikin's *Journal of a Tour through North Wales and part of Shropshire* (1797)

redder variation would have been commonly seen throughout Wales. They were colloquially referred to as 'runts' because of their small stature, but their hardy nature made them well suited to the rough grazing, heathland and mountainous terrain of Wales. It is estimated that by the beginning of the nineteenth century upwards of 30,000 Welsh Blacks were being exported annually. Although traditionally bred for both milk and meat, today they are used only for the latter, but in the time of the drovers they were also an important resource for other industries in England, providing the raw materials for craftsmen from girdlers and glovers to pouch-makers and tanners. Vast quantities of hides were exported from the towns strung along the coast of south Wales from Milford Haven all the way to Kidwelly.

In the Field

So how can we distinguish a drove route from, say, a farm track or a local bridle-path? Or, to put the question the other way round, what might the purpose of almost any thoroughfare originally have been apart from the droving of animals? For the vast majority of tracks, ways, lanes, minor and even major roads that we see today would have been used at some time in the past for the movement of livestock, over a variety of distances. It could be argued that most of the major roads out of Wales, especially those that run from west to east, would originally have been used for droving purposes, the example most frequently cited being the A44, which passes through Kington, Leominster, Bromyard and Worcester.

As previously mentioned, a useful definition of a drovers' road might be that it was used for the movement of livestock for the purpose of sale and not simply for reasons of animal husbandry or transhumance. Drovers' roads generally cover far greater distances than ways used for the more local movements of animals, and they tend to follow thoroughfares that are separate from the boundaries of local farms and enclosed fields, rather than going through or across them, although this is not true of older drove ways which predate field boundaries and the constrictions of the various Enclosure Acts. The routes usually head for places where drovers could find accommodation for themselves and grazing for their animals, though they generally avoid the centre of built-up areas, skirting the edges of towns and larger villages. And they tend to follow the higher ground, especially those that cross Wales. In short, almost all of the thread-like network of tracks and lanes to be found in Wales and the Marches would have been used at one time or another to drive animals from one place to another, although only a handful have evolved into the celebrated long-distance drovers' roads recognised today.

To investigate the local history of any area, we need to suspend our initial reaction to and interpretation of what we see in the landscape before us and try to imagine it as it was at a different

Pines by Strangworth Farm near Titley

time, in different social circumstances (although the more rural and wild a place is, the less necessary this is). We need to put ourselves into the mind and shoes of the drover, to try to contemplate what factors would be uppermost in his mind when deciding what route to take. His primary consideration can be summed up in one phrase: 'Time is money'. The longer the journey, the more wear and tear and the greater the cost of accommodation and subsistence for both men and beasts. Another principle, summed up in the phrase 'as-the-crow-flies', therefore also applies. But drovers were very much against false economies of any kind, and a compromise would always need to be made with the nature of the landscape and the arduousness of the terrain. Tiring animals unduly by making them climb hills that were too high or too hazardous, or risking losing them in a bog or swollen river, were obviously to be avoided no matter how straight or short the cut. Uplands were preferable for reasons of safety and the firm terrain they offered, but too much ascent and descent was to be avoided. Wide, gentle ridgeways were ideal, affording the vantage needed to see those markers in the landscape – the distinctive hills, pines and church spires – that signified the general direction to be taken. High routes also made it easier to spot the approach of any danger – highwaymen, cattle thieves, storm clouds, to name but a few. And, very importantly, they provided a solid surface across which to travel, in contrast to the quagmires that passed for roads in the valley bottoms. Where a ridge is particularly exposed to the elements, tracks tend to be found on the lee side of a hill, away from the prevailing direction of wind and adverse weather.

Rivers were the other major obstacle to the safe transport of animals. They had to be forded at some stage, but as seldom as possible, to minimise the loss of animals and the cost. At the most dangerous crossings, ferries especially provided for the task would have been used, the fare for men and beasts a necessary inconvenience weighed against the danger of trying to ford the river without them. A similar calculation would have been made concerning the outlay on accommodation, including stabling, fodder,

A ferry illustrated in W.H. Pyne's *The Costumes of Great Britain* (1808)

Whitney toll bridge

food and liquids for all and sundry. The inns that grew up along the main drove roads offered not just bed and board, but also safety in numbers for both the drover and his charges. However it was usually only the head-drover who would have been afforded the luxury of a bed for the night. More often than not his men would have to sleep close to the livestock in the stable or even in the lee of a hedge. From the 1700s onwards, the position of tollgates and turnpikes would also have influenced the route a drover would have taken, for they tried to avoid them as much as possible, rather than see their profits disappear into the pockets of tollgate keepers.

With all of these factors in mind, we can start to identify some of the key features in the landscape that might signify whether or not what we have before us is a thoroughfare that might have been used for droving at some time or another.

Place names

Names ascribed to a particular area, highway or habitation that are suggestive of droving origins include the following words and terms:

Halfpenny, referring to the money a drover would have been expected to pay to graze his animals overnight

Welshman's Lane (or other use of the word 'Welsh'), denoting a connection with Welsh drovers

Place-names like **Little London**, **Smithfield**, **Piccadilly**, **Hackney**, droving destinations in London after which drovers named their farms once they had retired and settled down, to remind themselves of their old droving days

The names of inns frequented by drovers, for example **Black Ox** and **Drovers Arms**

The use of such terms as biswal (dung) and stank (as in **Stanky Hill**, **Stanky Lane**)

There is also the famous **Welsh Road**, which ran all the way from north Wales, through Shrewsbury towards the south-east; and the **Welsh Way**, which left the Gloucester-Cirencester road near Duntisbourne eventually to meet the famous Ridgeway at Wantage before heading east towards London.

On the state of the roads

Between 1724 and 1727 Daniel Defoe made a tour 'through the whole isle of Great Britain', resulting in a series of books that commented on how he perceived the state of the nation. The following extracts concern the general state of the highways and the establishment of the new turnpikes and toll roads, which he wholeheartedly welcomed:

'So that upon the whole, this custom prevailing, 'tis more than probable, that our posterity may see the roads all over England restor'd in their time to such a perfection, that travelling and carriage of goods will be much more easy both to man and horse, than ever it was since the Romans lost this island.

Nor will the charge be burthensome to anybody; as for trade, it will be encourag'd by it every way; for carriage of all kind of heavy goods will be much easier, the waggoners will either perform in less time, or draw heavier loads, or the same load with fewer horses; the pack-horses will carry heavier burthens, or travel farther in a day, and so perform their journey in less time; all which will tend to lessen the rate of carriage, and so bring goods cheaper to market. The fat cattle will drive lighter, and come to market with less toil, and consequently both go farther in one day, and not waste their flesh, and heat and spoil themselves, in wallowing thro' the mud and sloughs, as is now the case. The sheep will be able to travel in the winter, and the city not be oblig'd to give great prizes to the butchers for mutton, because it cannot be brought up out of Leicestershire and Lincolnshire, the sheep not being able to travel: the graziers and breeders will not be oblig'd to sell their stocks of wethers [castrated male sheep] cheap in October to the farmers within 20 miles of London, because after that they cannot bring them up; but the ways being always light and sound, the graziers will keep their stocks themselves, and bring them up to market, as they see cause, as well in winter as in summer.'

In his story *The Two Drovers*, Walter Scott is describing Scots drovers, but they seem to have a lot in common with their Welsh counterparts:

Many large droves were about to set off for England, under the protection of their owners, or of the topsmen whom they employed in the tedious, laborious, and responsible office of driving the cattle for many hundred miles, from the market where they had been purchased, to the fields or farm-yards where they were to be fattened for the shambles.

The Highlanders in particular are masters of this difficult trade of driving, which seems to suit them as well as the trade of war. It affords exercise for all their habits of patient endurance and active exertion. They are required to know perfectly the drove-roads, which lie over the wildest tracts of the country, and to avoid as much as possible the highways, which distress the feet of the bullocks, and the turnpikes, which annoy the spirit of the drover; whereas on the broad green or grey track, which leads across the pathless moor, the herd not only move at ease and without taxation, but, if they mind their business, may pick up a mouthful of food by the way. At night, the drovers usually sleep along with their cattle, let the weather be what it will; and many of these hardy men do not once rest under a roof during a journey on foot from Lochaber to Lincolnshire. They are paid very highly, for the trust reposed is of the last importance, as it depends on their prudence, vigilance and honesty, whether the cattle reach the final market in good order, and afford a profit to the grazier. But as they maintain themselves at their own expense, they are especially economical in that particular. At the period we speak of, a Highland drover was victualled for his long and toilsome journey with a few handfuls of oatmeal and two or three onions, renewed from time to time, and a ram's horn filled with whisky, which he used regularly, but sparingly, every night and morning. His dirk, or *skene-dhu*, (i.e. black-knife,) so worn as to be concealed beneath the arm, or by the folds of the plaid, was his only weapon, excepting the cudgel with which he directed the movements of the cattle. A Highlander was never so happy as on these occasions. There was a variety in the whole journey, which exercised the Celt's curiosity and natural love of motion; there were the constant change of place and scene, the petty adventures incidental to the traffic, and the intercourse with the various farmers, graziers, and traders, intermingled with occasional merry-makings, not the less acceptable to Donald that they were void of expense; – and there was the consciousness of superior skill; for the Highlander, a child amongst flocks, is a prince amongst herds, and his natural habits induce him to disdain the shepherd's slothful life, so that he feels himself nowhere more at home than when following a gallant drove of his country cattle in the character of their guardian.

Pines and pond, Bailey Hill, near Knucklas

Pines, Ponds, Pounds and Pinfolds

Pines

The Scots Pine is the only species of pine native to northern Europe. It is fast-growing, can live for up to seven hundred years (although its average life-span is more likely to be around three hundred) and was ideal as a marker-tree, being evergreen and having such a distinctive shape. In the distant past the Scots Pine grew throughout mainland Britain, but it had to be reintroduced into England and Wales from Scotland after becoming extinct as a result of over-grazing, over-exploitation and over-use by Druids in their ceremonial bonfires and yuletide rituals. Alfred Watkins noted in *The Old Straight Track* that 'the Scotch fir is the typical tree of the ancient track'. Accounts of the use of pines by drovers as a reference point in the landscape are widespread, especially in Wales and Scotland, and it is the best-known and most extant indicator of drovers' roads in the landscape today. Pines occur on drove routes where you might most expect them: at the tops of hills and promontories, at crossroads and T-junctions, by field or farm. They commonly occur as a planting either of three or five. My surmise is that they were planted in such a way not only to show direction, but also to provide information regarding places to stop for board and/or grazing, and I would suggest that their specific number and positioning might have held some significance for our drover. However, the task for any researcher in the field is to distinguish the marker-pine from those in a landscape that may be there for other reasons, for example those that are naturally occurring, those that have been positioned as a windbreak, and that have been planted as mere ornamentation.

Ponds

A plentiful supply of water was as necessary as forage and fodder along drove roads. (The need for fodder meant that commons were also important.) Ponds found along drove roads on higher ground may be of the variety known as a dew-pond. The English word 'pool' is probably derived from the Welsh *pwll* and where it and the term 'cowpool' are used in lowland areas (instead of their English equivalents 'pond' and 'pit'), they may denote a route commonly used by drovers from Wales.

Pounds and Pinfolds
The terms 'pinfold' and 'pound' are Saxon in origin. (*Pundfald* and *pund* both meant an enclosure.) They were enclosed areas or structures in a village where stray animals that had been found on common grazing land were kept, only to be released on payment of a fine. For a small fee, these pounds were also used by drovers to pen animals overnight.

Highways and Byways
There are certain man-made tracks and thoroughfares in the landscape that are distinctive of drove routes. These include **hilltop tracks**, their sunken lanes showing the routes to which generations of animals were confined, so avoiding the dangers of bog and mire; similarly on drier high ground a collection of **wide tracks all heading in the same direction** and usually rendered bracken-free by the relentless treading of hooves; at lower levels, tracks that have **wider than usual verges** contained within distinct hedges or walls (many of these have been subsequently surfaced with tarmac and developed into minor and even major roads) or those known as **green lanes**, which have remained turfed; **roads and tracks that follow farm and estate boundaries** and/or provide links between fairs and markets; tracks that over time have become deeper, narrower lanes (also known as **hollow ways**), typically flanked by high-hedged embankments; tracks occasionally detected as **crop marks** or traced as **inundations** where modern cultivation may have eradicated original hedge and lane features. Tracks or hedges that come to the edge of a field and then seem to disappear completely might also signify more ancient **pre-enclosure ways**. Drovers are also said to have used preexisting **salt-routes**, especially in the counties of Cheshire and Staffordshire.

Railways and Railheads

The advent of the railway had a major influence on droving and drove routes. In the Marches the establishing of the railhead at Shrewsbury in 1848 (following the line's extension from Nuneaton) provides the first example of a railway's direct effect on the droving trade. Many drovers began to alter their routes, so that instead of crossing over the mountains of central Wales towards Hereford they moved north-east to Shrewsbury via the Welshpool area. By 1852 Craven Arms and Ludlow had also been reached by the railway, the line to Hereford itself was open a year later, and by 1857 Kington (via a link with Leominster) had a railhead for the 9,000 plus cattle that were estimated to arrive at the town annually. By 1865 the railway's tentacles had reached as far west as Knighton, Machynlleth and the Cardigan coast at Aberystwyth, so from that time on, cattle from mid-Wales had an even shorter journey to reach Shrewsbury and the rest of England. In this way the distances that drovers needed to drive animals became shorter and shorter, until, with the advent of the lorry, there was no need to travel on foot at all.

Tollgates and Turnpikes

The presence of a tollhouse or cottage is a good indicator that the road upon which it stands would have been used not only by coaches and travellers on horseback, but also by drovers and their animals at some earlier time. Their positioning on a thoroughfare (and that of their adjacent tollgates and turnpikes) was solely due to the amount of traffic on the route. It goes without saying that drovers objected to paying tolls and tried to avoid them if at all possible, even at the expense of an inconvenient detour, with time wasted and extra expenditure of energy, footwear and hoof. Conversely, there seem to have been many drovers who considered the tolls a necessary evil and were willing to pay them so as to arrive at market ahead of their rivals, and with their livestock in better fettle. There was no escaping the fact that the turnpike roads provided the most direct and eventually the best maintained routes into the heart of England. They were part of the general effort to improve the wellbeing and sanity of all travellers, an effort which is reflected in the fact that between 1760 and 1774 there were no less than 452 distinct Acts of Parliament passed with the specific aim of improving the state of the nation's roads. As Daniel Defoe argued in relation to the need for road improvements in Wales: 'The fat cattle will drive lighter, and come to market with less toil, and consequently both go farther in one day, and not waste their flesh, and heat and spoil themselves, in wallowing thro' the mud and sloughs, as is now the case.'

Roadside Industries

Over the centuries the droving of animals through the Welsh Marches and the English countryside resulted in the creation of several important roadside industries, evidence of which still exists today and can thus denote a drove route. At the peak of droving, between the 1750s and the 1850s, drovers would have produced livelihoods for thousands of people in the areas through which they passed. Smithies were needed for shoeing (when it came to cattle, because of their cloven hooves, each animal required eight separate shoes), farms and landowners provided pasture and fodder, and inns offered the drovers food and lodging. It is estimated that over half the expenses that a drover incurred related to feeding his animals. This was especially the case in England, where the gradual enclosure of common land and restriction of access to riverbanks meant that finding free pasture and water was increasingly difficult. Drovers could also suffer greater expense at or near fairs and markets, where animals might have to be kept and fed for a number of days prior to a sale.

Minor occupations associated with droving included ferrymen and boys; travelling blacksmiths, who accompanied the larger droves; and hired hands, including local boys, if extra help was needed to cross open mountainside or to guard animals overnight, especially at market. There was also a wide variety of industries and occupations that relied on the by-products of animals – for example, tanners, saddle-makers and an assortment of other craftsmen who depended on hides and leather; soap makers, who used the animals' fat; makers of utensils that involved horn and bone; and plaster-workers who used animal hair – to name but a few. With the demise of droving in late Victorian times, all of these trades and industries were affected and many of them severely, some to the point of becoming extinct.

Mr. Bos

George Borrow meets a drover in the White Horse tavern

In 1858 the traveller and writer George Borrow journeyed the length and breadth of Wales, and recorded his journey in his famous book Wild Wales. *The following extract tells of his meeting with a drover by the name of Bos in the White Horse tavern, Pentraeth Coch:*

I arrived at the hostelry of Mr. Pritchard without meeting any adventure worthy of being marked down. I went into the little parlour, and, ringing the bell, was presently waited upon by Mrs. Pritchard, a nice matronly woman, whom I had not before seen, of whom I inquired what I could have for dinner ...

Having made arrangements for "boxing Harry" [i.e. a snack rather than a dinner] I went into the tap-room, from which I had heard the voice of Mr. Pritchard proceeding during the whole of my conversation with his wife. Here I found the worthy landlord seated with a single customer; both were smoking. The customer instantly arrested my attention. He was a man seemingly about forty years of age with a broad red face, with certain somethings, looking very much like incipient carbuncles, here and there upon it. His eyes were grey and looked rather as if they squinted; his mouth was very wide, and when it opened displayed a set of strong white, uneven teeth. He was dressed in a pepper-and-salt coat of the Newmarket cut, breeches of corduroy and brown top boots, and had on his head a broad, black, coarse, low-crowned hat. In his left hand he held a heavy white whale-bone whip with a brass head. I sat down on a bench nearly opposite to him and the landlord.

"Well," said Mr. Pritchard; "did you find your way to Llanfair?"

"Yes," said I.

Sylvanus Evans (1833-1911),
drover of Llan Ffestiniog, Merioneth

"And did you execute the business satisfactorily which led you there?" said Mr. Pritchard.

"Perfectly," said I.

"Well, what did you give a stone for your live pork?" said his companion, glancing up at me, and speaking in a gruff voice.

"I did not buy any live pork," said I; "do you take me for a pig-jobber?"

"Of course," said the man in pepper-and-salt; "who but a pig-jobber could have business at Llanfair?"

"Does Llanfair produce nothing but pigs?" said I.

"Nothing at all," said the man in the pepper-and-salt; "that is nothing worth mentioning. You wouldn't go there for runts, that is if you were in your right senses; if you were in want of runts you would have gone to my parish and have applied to me, Mr. Bos; that is if you were in your senses. Wouldn't he, John Pritchard?"

Mr. Pritchard thus appealed to took the pipe out of his mouth, and with some hesitation said that he believed the gentleman neither went to Llanfair for pigs nor black cattle but upon some particular business.

"Well," said Mr. Bos, "it may be so, but I can't conceive how any person, either gentle or simple, could have any business in Anglesey save that business was pigs or cattle."

"The truth is," said I, "I went to Llanfair to see the

birth-place of a great man – the cleverest Anglesey ever produced."

"Then you went wrong," said Mr. Bos, "you went to the wrong parish, you should have gone to Penmynnydd; the clebber man of Anglesey was born and buried at Penmynnydd; you may see his tomb in the church."

"You are alluding to Black Robin," said I, "who wrote the ode in praise of Anglesey – yes, he was a very clever young fellow, but excuse me, he was not half such a poet as Gronwy Owen."

"Black Robin," said Mr. Bos, "and Gronow Owen, who the Devil were they? I never heard of either. I wasn't talking of them, but of the clebberest man the world ever saw. Did you never hear of Owen Tiddir? If you didn't, where did you get your education?"

"I have heard of Owen Tudor," said I, "but never understood that he was particularly clever; handsome he undoubtedly was – but clever –"

"How not clebber?" interrupted Mr. Bos. "If he wasn't clebber, who was clebber? Didn't he marry a great queen, and was not Harry the Eighth his great grandson?"

"Really," said I, "you know a great deal of history."

"I should hope I do," said Mr. Bos. "O, I wasn't at school at Blewmaris for six months for nothing; and I haven't been in Northampton, and in every town in England without learning something of history. With regard to history I may say that few. Won't you drink?" said he, patronizingly, as he pushed a jug of ale which stood before him on a little table towards me.

Begging politely to be excused on the plea that I was just about to take tea, I asked him in what capacity he had travelled all over England.

"As a drover, to be sure," said Mr. Bos, "and I may say that there are not many in Anglesey better known in England than myself – at any rate I may say that there is not a public-house between here and Worcester at which I am not known."

"Pray excuse me," said I, "but is not droving rather a low-lifed occupation?"

"Not half so much as pig-jobbing," said Bos, "and that that's your trade I am certain, or you would never have gone to Llanfair."

"I am no pig-jobber," said I, "and when I asked you that question about droving, I merely did so because one Ellis Wynn, in a book he wrote, gives the drovers a very bad character, and puts them in Hell for their mal-practices."

"O, he does," said Mr. Bos, "well the next time I meet him at Corwen I'll crack his head for saying so. Mal-practices – he had better look at his own, for he is a pig-jobber too. Written a book has he? then I suppose he has been left a legacy, and gone to school after middle-age, for when I last saw him, which is four years ago, he could neither read nor write."

I was about to tell Mr. Bos that the Ellis Wynn that I meant was no more a pig-jobber than myself, but a respectable clergyman, who had been dead considerably upwards of a hundred years, and that also, notwithstanding my respect for Mr. Bos's knowledge of history, I did not believe that Owen Tudor was buried at Penmynnydd, when I was prevented by the entrance of Mrs. Pritchard, who came to inform me that my repast was ready in the other room, whereupon I got up and went into the parlour to "box Harry".

Tired at length with my vain efforts to account for the term which in my time was so much in vogue amongst commercial gentlemen I left the little parlour, and repaired to the common room. Mr. Pritchard and Mr. Bos were still there smoking and drinking, but there was now a candle on the table before them, for night was fast coming on. Mr. Bos was giving an account of his travels in England, sometimes in Welsh, sometimes in English, to which Mr. Pritchard was listening with the greatest attention, occasionally putting in a "see there now," and "what a fine thing it is to have gone about." After some time Mr. Bos exclaimed:

"I think, upon the whole, of all the places I have seen in England I like Northampton best."

"I suppose," said I, "you found the men of Northampton good-tempered, jovial fellows?"

"Can't say I did," said Mr. Bos; "they are all shoemakers, and of course quarrelsome and contradictory, for where was there ever a shoemaker who was not conceited and easily riled? No, I have little to say in favour of Northampton, as far as the men are concerned. It's not the men but the women that make me speak in praise of Northampton. The men are all ill-tempered, but the women quite the contrary. I never saw such a place for *merched anladd* as Northampton. I was a great favourite with them, and could tell you such tales."

And then Mr. Bos putting his hat rather on one side of his head told us two or three tales of his adventures with the *merched anladd* of Northampton, which brought powerfully to mind part of what Ellis Wynn had said with respect to the practices of drovers in his day, detestation for which had induced him to put the whole tribe into Hell. ...

Time passed, night came on, and other guests came in. There was much talking of first-rate Welsh and very indifferent English, Mr. Bos being the principal speaker in both languages; his discourse was chiefly on the comparative merits of Anglesey runts and Scotch bullocks, and those of the *merched anladd* of Northampton and the lasses of Wrexham. He preferred his own country runts to the Scotch kine, but said upon the whole, though a Welshman, he must give a preference to the *merched* of Northampton over those of Wrexham, for free-and-easy demeanour, notwithstanding that in that point which he said was the most desirable point in females, the lasses of Wrexham were generally considered out-and-outers.

'Flying with the high fields' between Knighton and Clun

Huw the Drover

Huw Pritchard, Welsh drover, cattle dealer, a man of Tregaron born and bred with 67 years to heaven and a farmstead to his name, awoke to the dawn's early light and the song of a blackbird carried in on a gentle breeze from the tall elm wind-break outside the window. For an hour or so he had been dozing, moving in and out of sleep, thinking about the day ahead and the drove that would be his very last, and dreaming about his retirement and the wide beach at Aberaeron bay with a boat out in the harbour, the one with the name *Ceri* written along its side. Dreaming about the distant past and the girl who was now his wife, the girl he had known since he could first remember walking with his mother through the sunlight to the chapel and its wondrous parables of a Sunday morn. Seeing her with her parents cross the street ahead of them, looking back over her shoulder and then ... that glance, that smile. The one who was wont to say he would be dreaming even if he was wide awake and standing on two legs in the high field at noon. Huw smiled to himself and instinctively put a hand out to feel her still-sleeping warmth by his side.

The dawn chorus continued to fill him, first one song, a robin's, and then another and another, until it seemed his whole body was brimming with birdsong from head to toe, and the sweet song was spilling out and filling the entire room. It was then that he opened his eyes and in one swift movement sidled out of bed and moved towards the window he always liked to have slightly ajar. He opened it wide and looked with a knowing eye across the sky. Some cloud was still moving in from the west, but it was much lighter than the evening before and all the signs suggested that the day would be a decent one, free of rain. Huw moved back into the room then and began the well-honed process that would see him within half an hour prepared and on horseback ready for the drove.

At 6.25am he opened the large oak front door, the one he had reclaimed from his father's abandoned hafod high up on the hill some twenty years back, and stepped out into the cobbled yard. The morning was now a bright one and the view down the valley and across towards the mountain was as clear as he could have hoped for on a first day's drive. Huw could just make out the route they would be taking in an hour or so's time, up through the pass above Cwm Berwyn, where the sun itself was just rising, and over the hills to Abergwesyn. Bringing his horse out from the stable, he went back in at the neighed request of Cysgod, the 14-year-old that he had never been able to part with even when he was offered ten guineas that time down at Rugby fair. He patted her side as if to say 'Just wait till I get back', for she was desperate to go, but had driven her last cattle a few seasons back. This journey would be taken with her stablemate, Idris.

Having secured his travelling bag, he was ready to set off down the lane to meet his son and the other two men who would already be set to depart. They were good men all three and could be relied upon. He was just about to take the stirrup when he heard a call from behind. It was Ceri, with one last kiss for the road and a parcel of food for the day ahead. She had seen it all before of course, but still it felt hard knowing that the best part of two weeks would have to be spent without him. For her it never seemed to get any easier, though she had never let him know. This time, however, felt different, for she really believed it would be the last drove, now that Dafydd, their firstborn and the eldest of three, had reached the age of 40, the age when a married man with land to his name was legally able to take up the reins of a business that had been in their family for four generations now at least. Maybe even longer. Huw's grandfather used to argue that droving had been in the blood of his forefathers even when the monks walked the cloisters at Strata Florida Abbey on the other side of the big hill. On that bright October morn, the 26th of the month, 1814, as father and son made their final preparations, how were they to know that Dafydd would be the last in the line? For a man by the name of Stephenson would that very day put the finishing pencil marks to his design for the 'steam-powered horse' that in a generation would bring an end to the trade of droving as they knew it.

The cattle lay penned before them, 372 'runts', all felled and branded in the previous three days. On this occasion Johnny Jones and his gang had been assigned the task. Old Probert was too old for this kind of work any more and had gone to live with his sister in Lampeter on account of his wife having passed away the year before. As for a fresh shoeing, Huw had plans for that on reaching Kington, for the journey there was largely over soft ground and even the coach roads in this part of the world were largely unmetalled.

There were also a handful of milch cows to accompany them, so that the two hired hands – Dewi Edwards and Taffy Griffiths – could make a bit of extra money on the roadside selling to the goodwives and school kids that requested their cream-rich fare.

It was with a loud 'Haiptarw ho!' that Huw led the procession of animals and men out from the pound behind the Talbot and up the old drove road east to the crest of the cwm. Here he turned back to look one last time to his farm on the other side of the valley, so small against the hill, where he could just make out a figure hanging out washing along a line. Even further into the distance, below the far horizon, the shining sea merged with the sky, and Huw was sure he could just make out a boat, a small one, with her name writ along its side. He paused for a second until he heard Dafydd at the front cajoling a loose cow, at which he turned and headed with the rest down into the first of the countless valleys that made up the noble land that he was proud to call his home.

Down in the bottom where the Afon Berwyn was met by the Afon Cammdwr they crossed a ford. Here the animals were allowed to slake their thirst, a pause that gave Huw the opportunity to check the other men had settled in and to enjoy the wild valleys that rose all around him. To the north an ancient monks' trod led up to the abbey ruins of Strata Florida, a route used by countless drovers which continued south up to the place his grandfather was known to take himself whenever the inner call took him and the need arose for time away from the company of others to be alone, just him and his God. Like those wandering saints of old, Huw thought to himself, and he remembered the last words his grandfather had ever spoken to him: "We drove animals because it has always been this way, for as far back as any of us can remember, as our fathers and grandfathers have done, following the cattle from Cardigan Bay to Rhydspence Inn and then down through Herefordshire. We are drovers because it is in our blood and being on the road lifts our hearts and makes our spirits sing … it is part of who we are as a people."

Huw turned to the road ahead. It wasn't a bad one as roads went, for he had rarely known it to be impassable, except in the deepest mid-winter when no man or beast should have call to come this way. It also avoided the turnpikes that had been strung along all the main river valleys and townships, though if the men of Rhayader he'd heard about had anything to do with it, they wouldn't be a bugbear for too much longer. 'Rebecca and her daughters', they called themselves, and Huw knew his Bible well enough to know the reference: to Rebecca in the Book of Genesis, who spoke of 'possessing the gates of those who hate them'.

Huw reckoned on eventually setting a pace of between fifteen and twenty miles' progress a day. However, the first halt was always Abergwesyn's Grouse Inn, which, being just shy of thirteen miles' tread, meant that the first day's journey was never going to be overly strenuous. As Huw figured it, the right pace and tone for both mind and muscle had to be found from the outset. The Grouse also happened to be a place Huw had come to know well over the years, where he was always welcomed and the food and board was better than most. Having checked the cattle, Huw arranged for Dafydd and himself to room inside. The other two men would be with the animals, keeping watch with the dogs and saving their daily wage of three shillings. Huw was known in Tregaron for looking out for his hired hands and they knew there would be a decent six-shilling bonus at the end if all went to plan. He had even given them a pair of gaiters each, for he always considered it good business in the long-term to keep the men on his side and treat them as he had expected to be treated back when he had first started driving animals, during the lean months of the year when the farm was quiet and the lads were old enough to help their mother around the place.

Before turning in, Huw stepped outside to smoke his pipe and to take in the stars and the crescent moon that hung high in the sky, his stomach and spirit now pleasantly pacified by a mixture of beer, bread and stewed mutton. He got into talking with a hosier-man from Newquay who was heading east with a few mules loaded with stockings and gloves. Huw offered him the company of his drove, but the man was going a different way, to Worcester via Rhydspence and Hereford. In the past Huw had escorted all manner of folk to the big cities, from farm girls going into service to the sons of gentry off to work with their uncles. He had even been asked once to take some 'Ship Money', raised from taxes gathered down in Milford Haven. Though the fee would have been useful, Huw had declined on several counts: he was unsure about the highwaymen at that time, especially down on the Surrey heaths, and he had come close the year before to a place where a Cardy man had been robbed and beaten badly; he didn't have much time for these government men and their officialdom, but about that he maintained the less said the better; and he didn't take to the agent himself for, though of Welsh blood, he seemed to have lost the use of his mother tongue.

The next morning over breakfast Huw hired a local lad for the next stage of the journey, to bring back to the herd any cattle that strayed too far on the expanse of high ground that lay ahead, between Abergwesyn and Beulah village in the Wye valley beyond. The route initially followed a hedged lane out of the village rising up to the Cefn Cardis ('Cardiganshire Ridge') before widening out onto the barren hilltop where the hireling would come into his own. The problem of cattle wandering was balanced by the potential bonus of absorbing animals from the herds of those farms they passed by on their long journey, and there were some drovers who weren't against a bit of excess swelling their stock. Huw wasn't one of them, for he had found that it was not worth the strain on temper and time to provoke the ire of local farmers and risk the delays their confabulations caused.

From Beulah they headed north-east on a well-defined road past the Red Lion at Llanafan-fawr (where a glass of cider had to be had) on to Newbridge-on-Wye, where Huw decided to halt for the night and make use of the lush pasture of the river meadows that lay close by. The libations on offer at the Mid-Wales Tavern would also not go amiss. That evening Huw began the notes that he would later transcribe into his ledger, which would comprise his final entries in that renowned volume. Huw's book-keeping was well regarded in the inns and fairs of Tregaron, both for the fastidiousness with which he detailed the transactions of the many droves he had taken and for the fine flourish of his hand. Not every dealer of animals in that part of Wales could write and of those that could, hardly a one could match Huw Pritchard's tidy pen, a legacy he could thank his grandfather for.

Day three saw the drove continuing north-west to Llandrindod Wells, where Huw had to pay out thirteen shillings and sixpence to a local farmer for grass, the animals being unable to find enough sustenance on the waysides in that area. They then completed the seventeen miles to the Fforest Inn at Llanfihangel, where he paid out a further sixteen shillings for grass and six shillings for their accommodation. The inn stood on the main highway that headed from west to east through the mountains on the other side of which lay Herefordshire and England. The road would take them through Kington, Leominster, Bromyard and eventually to Worcester and beyond into the farmlands of Northamptonshire. From now on the costs would mount, as everything was more expensive in England. But for Huw, on his last ever drove and with an old man's legs, it was a price worth paying. It would also bring the beasts to his buyer in better condition, for less toil meant less 'bloom' on their hides, caused by the successive coats of sweat drying each day. The trick, he knew, was to vary the stages whenever possible, a strenuous one followed by an easier day: a balance in all things, as Mother Nature and his Sunday schooling in the chapel had taught him.

The following morning they encountered their first tollgate a few miles down the road at Maesyfed (commonly known as New Radnor) – the price one shilling and sixpence. Six miles further on, they crossed the border into Herefordshire to the north of Kington. In the past Huw might have considered avoiding its gate (three shillings) by going the long way around, up over Rushock Hill and down through Titley. However, the animals desperately needed shoeing (which cost a guinea), so that they could cope with the metalled roads that lay ahead, and Kington was the best place for it. During the stop they would also need grass (eighteen shillings). But Huw considered bed and board too pricy in the town, and opted to head a few miles further east before the night's fall, to a place he knew near Lynhales. From this point on, the days would see them taking in more miles, for the road would be almost arrow-straight and the terrain predominantly flat compared to what they were accustomed to back in their homeland.

The next day was the longest so far, over twenty miles to Westington gate (three shillings), which stood just beyond Docklow, about half-way between Leominster and Bromyard. Here Huw paid out for two lots of grass (ten shillings and five shillings and ninepence), the one farmer not having sufficient for his needs. In the past he would have used the downs at Bromyard, but since the Enclosure Acts free grazing had become increasingly hard to find this side of the border, and the commons were less accessible to the Welsh drovers. That evening being a dry and a fair one, all four men stayed the night around a fire under the stars, trading stories and singing songs. It was something Huw had done more frequently in the past and he was glad in his heart to have spent this occasion on his final drove with his son and the men he had known for many a year now. 'Just like the old days,' he sighed contentedly before turning into his blanket by the fireside.

Huw had decided to make Day 6 easier on all, just over ten miles, ending at Bontwillt Tavern (seventeen shillings and threepence), a favourite of his that he knew took kindly to drovers. By noon they had passed the Bromyard gate (three shillings and sixpence) and four hours later arrived at Bontwillt gate (two shillings and threepence). Checking the animals, Taffy Morris discovered one with a large cut down her flank. Fortunately Huw always made sure that one of his hired hands had some veterinary skills, over and above the basics that most drovers had. On this drove Dewi Edwards was the man. He had learnt from his grandmother the way of healing with country herbs and plants and was well regarded by his fellow Cardis for his poultices and unctions. After cleaning the wound, he applied a paste largely consisting of the dried thyme and sage he always carried with him and the comfrey leaves and flowers of the John's wort he had picked up from the wayside. Also there was the mystery powder he seemed to brandish on any and every occasion, whose substance and origins his grinning face would never reveal, even after an hour of the digging and teasing which his side-kick, Taffy, was often wont to try.

The next day was a long one, twenty-five miles or so. It found them by late morning heading through Worcester's west gate (three shillings), a place too busy by half for Huw. They stopped at a tavern on its outskirts for lunch (six shillings), before making their way through the east gate (two shillings and sixpence) towards their halt for the night at Wilbercastle (gate two shillings and threepence, tavern eighteen shillings). Huw avoided the centres of the larger towns if he could help it, the attitude of the local populace to the Welsh drovers being uncertain and sometimes even confrontational the further you ventured into England. In the past it was not such a problem, and he had escorted plenty of droves through places like Hereford and Worcester in his younger days before he led them himself, and was known to give as good as he got. But some of the young men of the towns, especially those idling outside the inns and cider houses, were wont to spook the cattle for the sheer hell of it, and a stampede in such a place was the last thing Huw wanted.

In the evening Huw got talking to a local shepherd about the droving trade and how many dealers had recently changed how they purchased their animals. Many now went straight to the hill farmers direct, or were visited by the farmers at some agreed lowland location, or even on the drove route itself. The smaller dealers would also take animals on credit, especially from farmers with smallholdings in isolated places far from even the nearest hamlet. Huw had done so himself when he had first started out, but now he had the capital to pay for the animals up front and could carry the occasional loss here and there, for he knew that by the end of the season there was always be a profit to be had.

They spent a good hour or so drinking the local cider as they mulled over the fairs they had enjoyed in their time. Huw told the shepherd about the biggest he could remember, the Cilgerran May Fair of 1805. 'Aye, that was a good time, cattle lining the street from the rectory to the coach station and spilling out into the fields all round the town.' 40,000 plus, according to old Evan Evans, his father's head drover, now deceased, 'though who could say, for who was a-counting?' Business had been brisk and all was sealed and done with by the one o'clock bell, so presenting an afternoon of chewing the cud and drinking at the watering hole, the White Horse tavern on Mill Street. This had been Huw's favourite haunt – well, at that time of day at least, for a score of others would be visited in the course of the fair if not by the end of the day. The best of times, they both concluded, the best of times indeed.

On the seventh day they found themselves heading the eight miles east to Stratford, which they reached by the early afternoon (gate two shillings and sixpence, tavern three shillings, grass fourteen shillings and sixpence). After men and beasts had had their fill, they carried on the nine miles north-east to Warwick (gate two shillings and threepence, tavern eighteen shillings and sixpence) and its Angel Inn, where they halted for the night. It was then that Dewi Edwards noticed that one of his two dogs, a corgi by the name of Siabod, was missing. She was a young dog, this being only her second drove, but it was still a loss, for she had a good way with the animals and they all agreed had shown the potential to turn out well.

Huw himself had always favoured a collie. The present one was eight years old, and he had to admit she had become more of a pet than he would have liked. Though the corgis were a better height for running between the legs of the runts and nipping their ankles, especially when they had packed together, there was none like his collie for working his small flock of speckled-faced sheep. Anyway, he had kept enough corgis in his time and had left the two he had now at home with Ceri. They had done their time; it was now the job of Dafydd's dogs to lead the way. As for Dewi's lost corgi, there was always the chance that she would find her own way home. This wasn't unknown among the drovers, but none of the three men had experienced it, and they all agreed that it was a feat that would be more likely to be achieved by a collie dog than a corgi.

The next day was their eighth and last full day on the road, for the stockman's farm was situated fifteen miles or so further on, south-east of Southam. It was uneventful, which is how Huw liked it, and had been

Cilgerran Fair c.1885

planned to be as short as possible so that the animals would not be strained and could look their best. They made a halt in the late afternoon, eleven miles on, by the Windmill gate (two shillings) east of Southam, making use of the tavern of the same name (eighteen shillings). They had to make an early start on the morning of the ninth day, for as well as delivering their charges, the drovers had to cover a substantial distance back towards Tregaron before nightfall. Huw had settled up with the landlord at the Windmill the evening before, so by 6am they were setting out along the old Welsh Road that ran all the way from the Black Country to the Home Counties, towards their rendezvous with the farmer who would fatten up the stock ready for sale the following spring.

To Huw's mind, as English farmers went, Mr. Agnew wasn't a bad sort and seemed to have more respect for the sons of Cymru than a few others he had encountered over the years. Dafydd would continue to do business with Agnew and then his son for another twenty-seven seasons, until his own retirement. But he would be the last in the line, for his wife Rhiannon would never be blessed with the children they longed for, though a distant cousin would continue droving between Breconshire and Hereford well into the 1920s. And then, of course, there were the railways, whose tentacles, within fifty years of Huw's last drove, would have spread as far west as Tregaron itself, where a station officially opened on a September day in 1866. Little did father and son know that from that moment on, the droving trade they and the forefathers had plied for countless miles under countless moons and suns would begin to dwindle steadily away. Within a century it would have disappeared altogether, to become just a memory in the minds of a few and the subject of books and academic papers.

Three days later, father and son passed back through the cwm to find spread out below them the valley of their birth and the western sun shimmering over the distant sea. They paused to take in the view, before Huw slapped his son tenderly on the back and, pointing Idris towards the descent below, started the final leg home. Just over an hour later he was back in the arms of Ceri, whose embrace was as sweet as he could ever remember it. They were never to spend more than a night apart again, the rest of their lives being lived together as if they were still the childhood sweethearts who had shared that glance all those years back.

Part Two
Walking the Drovers' Roads

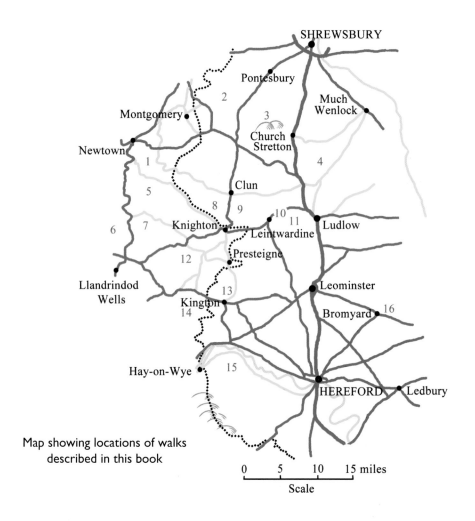

Map showing locations of walks described in this book

SHREWSBURY

Pontesbury

Much Wenlock

2

Montgomery

3

Church Stretton

4

Newtown

1

5

Clun

8   9

10

11

Knighton

Leintwardine

Ludlow

6   7

Presteigne

12

Llandrindod Wells

13

Leominster

Kington

14

Bromyard   16

Hay-on-Wye

15

HEREFORD   Ledbury

0   5   10   15 miles

Scale

Key to maps accompanying walk descriptions.
Places and features marked on the maps are in bold text when first mentioned in the descriptions.
Not all the walks begin at designated car parks but in all cases there are places to park nearby; please take care to park your car safely and considerately.

—— A road
—— B road
—— Other tarmacked road
▓ Woodland
—— Stream or river
– Building or group of buildings
— Indication of slope from hill top
— Line of walk
— Other paths
① Point on map relating to same point in walk description
🍺 Pub

Section 1
Welshpool and Montgomery to Shrewsbury

At the village of Forden, south of Welshpool, where an ancient ford once crossed the wandering river Severn, an important drovers' road is said by Richard Moore-Colyer (in his *Roads and Trackways of Wales*) to be joined by a long-distance route used for centuries by cattle drovers arriving from north-west Wales and fish traders from the villages that line Cardigan Bay. From Forden (SJ233011) the drove route continues across the Long Mountain to Shrewsbury, still following the course of the Roman road that runs north from Montgomery. Initially it follows the present-day B4388, then the Roman Road (SJ246032) that passes the onetime drovers' inn known as the Welsh Harp (SJ277080), before going on to Westbury, where it becomes the B4386. It would probably have been joined at places along its course by other drovers' roads heading east out of the hills around Welshpool.

On reaching Shrewsbury drovers took the Welsh Road – the main route down though the Midlands to the markets and fairs of the south-east – along the old paved Roman road known as Watling Street. It originally passed through Wroxeter, 5 miles south-east of Shrewsbury and the site of the fourth largest Roman settlement in Britain, Viroconium. From there it continued over Cannock Chase to Brownhills, where it followed the present-day A452 to Castle Bromwich, Kenilworth and then towards Buckingham. At Brownhills another important drove route headed south along what is now the A5 to London.

The Kerry Ridgeway to Shrewsbury
The famous Kerry Ridgeway (**Walk 1**), which rises south of Newtown, continues to radiate history and pre-history along the entire 16 miles it takes to reach Bishop's Castle, a town which retains a cattle market to this day. The Kerry Ridgeway's elevated views and panorama make it one of the most

Looking towards the Kerry Ridgeway close to Medwaledd

dramatic drovers' roads in the whole of the Marches, if not the whole country. It begins at the Cider House (SO108846), a well-renowned onetime drovers' inn originally known as New Pound, with its solitary pine pointing the direction to be taken up towards the ridge itself. The Two Tumps – those mammary tumuli that face heavenwards from their resting place upon the earth – are the first features encountered as you achieve the high ground. It is said that the Ridgeway which passes them is far older even than these, the first feet and hooves that trod there being lost in unrecorded time.

A few miles west of Bishop's Castle, at an important crossroads on the ridgeway, lies Dog and Duck Cottage, once an inn used by the drovers. On reaching the town itself, it is likely that one drove route would have headed in a north-easterly direction towards Shrewsbury and the A5 along the valley of the river East Onny. This route follows the present-day minor road that goes through Lydham Heath, Norbury, Gravenor, Bridges, Pulverbatch, Longden Common and Annscroft.

Further back along the Kerry Ridgeway there is another likely drove route that begins its descent at Pantglas (SO247896) to cross the valley west towards Churchstoke, before continuing north-west (**Walk 2**) between Green and Old Church Stoke via Chasleyfield Farm (SO945277). It then carries on across the road to then rise up to pass between Lan Fawr and Corndon Hill, where it eventually meets the Priest Weston-White Grit road which rises up from Chirbury on a route drovers might also have followed east from Montgomery. This it crosses to continue in its north-westerly direction by Mitchell's Fold stone circle, where it then diverts (at SJ312992) to follow the base of the hill and arrive at the footpath that passes between Bromlow Callow and the hill with the old cracked trig-point lying adjacent to it.

If ever there was a distinctive drovers' landmark visible from miles around, then it has to be the group of hilltop pines of Bromlow Callow (SJ325011) south-west of Pontesbury. This large clump of trees presented an important navigation point on the drovers' road that led in a north-westerly direction from the Kerry Ridgeway and Bishop's Castle, to the markets and rail sidings of Shrewsbury. A place for gathering and resting, only a day's droving from their destination, the area around the 'callow' provided several water sources within a large expanse of common ground for rough grazing, as well as the prospect of better pasture and accommodation at the adjacent Hope Park Farm. From here the route continues downhill along the minor road via Hopesgate and its drovers' pub, the Stables Inn (SJ338017), towards Plox Green and Minsterley, before eventually arriving in the vicinity of the county town itself. There are also intriguing pines at the Alport crossroads (SO273953), just north of Churchstoke.

Bishop's Castle to Church Stretton and Craven Arms

Originally a farmhouse built in 1670, the Six Bells pub lies at the point where the drovers' road (which follows the present-day Kerry Lane) joins Bishop's Castle's main street. It became a hostelry in 1750 to offer accommodation and paddocks for the increasing number of drovers arriving in the town after their long trek through Wales. After enjoying what delights Bishop's Castle offered, drovers had two routes to choose from as they headed east. The first and the oldest would have passed over the Long Mynd down towards Shrewsbury, with a diversion heading towards Much Wenlock and the Black Country. The second route had a closer destination in the form of Craven Arms, a town which really came into its own when the railway arrived and quite literally put the place on the map.

To reach the Long Mynd at the southern entrance to the Port Way (that most ancient of Mynd drove routes, which traces its entire hogsback length), drovers would most likely have taken the road which leaves the town at its north-west corner and crosses the A488 at SO330893, before heading east (note the milestones) via Totterton and Eyton to cross over the river Onny at Plowden. Like the Kerry Ridgeway, the Port Way (**Walk 3**) is said to have been used as early as 4000BC by Neolithic axe-traders, and then as a Kings Highway well into the Middle Ages. There are a score of tracks that branch from it as it traverses the entire length of the Long Mynd, the major ones being the two that drop down to Minton and Little Stretton; the Burway road (SO424945), which drops down into Church Stretton; and the path which begins at SO435967 to descend into All Stretton. Otherwise the route would have continued northwards to Shrewsbury, via Woolstaston, Burgs hillfort and Sutton Hall, eventually to cross the river Severn at Robertsford.

To get to Craven Arms from Bishop's Castle the drovers would have taken the aptly named Stank Lane (see page 19), which ascends Oakeley Mynd from where it leaves the sharp bend of the B4385

Between Helmeth and Hope Bowdler hills, Church Stretton

Between Adstone and Medlicott, towards the Long Mynd

at SO332877 by a cottage that may at one time have been a toll-house. This present-day minor road, a ridgeway in its own right, progresses up Basford Bank to skirt around Wart Hill (SO401847) and enter Craven Arms from the north along Long Lane. At Edgton there is another possible drove route that might have headed north-east along the minor road that skirts Ridgeway Hill and crosses the river Onny by Horderley Farm, where it follows the A489 for a hundred yards or so before continuing in a north-easterly direction along the road that passes Cwm Head to Marshbrook. Here the route crosses the A49 to ascend either through the cwm towards the high road west of Oakwood or to The Common, a place which only appears on older maps, but is denoted today by the group of pines which stand at the Acton Scott crossroads (SO454900). There may also have been a drove way that departed the minor road from Edgton just before Ridgeway Farm (SO396864) to follow the public footpath that descends Ridgeway Hill by Castle Ring to the ford at Horderley. From there it would have headed north to the left of Bank Farm (SO408873) along the main track to Hamperley, where it becomes the present-day minor road that leads to Minton, Little Stretton and beyond.

Local features that indicate drovers' roads:
Pines – SO343874; SO350874; SO401847; SO405845; SO432907
Places – Red House Farm SO365861; Hammondsgreen SO405845; Manor Farm SO432907

East of Church Stretton
Apart from the well documented routes mentioned above that cross the Long Mynd, there are also many green lanes and 'hollow ways' said to have been used by drovers further east on the famous Wenlock Edge. Between them, however, on the other side of the Stretton fault, runs another ridge of high ground between Ragleth Hill and The Lawley, where a substantial track might represent another drove route heading north-west towards Much Wenlock, Telford and the Wrekin. Like the Mynd and the Edge, it too is criss-crossed with smaller tracks that intersect and join each other at various places. To begin with, it follows the eastern slope of the hills along the minor road that runs north of Acton Scott via The Hough

Example of a hollow way (this one ascending Merbach Hill)

and Dryhill Farm, before dropping down to the B4371 at SO469933. This it crosses to continue as the track that skirts Helmeth Hill to meet the drove way coming up from Church Stretton at the footbridge (SO472943). From here the route heads north-east via Cwms Cottage to Willstone Farm and then right along the minor road that follows Yell Bank Ridge via Holme Farm, and descends into Church Preen, Hughley before climbing up onto Wenlock Edge. There would also have been a drove way that joins this one at SO497962, rising up from All Stretton and Leebotwood, the latter with its onetime pound and Pound Inn (now known simply as The Pound), which is said to have been a drovers' hostelry.

However, it seems likely that the main drove road that crosses Ape Dale towards the Edge and thence to Much Wenlock would have continued west and north from the Acton Scott crossroads along the present-day roads that go via Hatton, Ticklerton, Wall, Longville and Presthope. It is probable that a minor route would have left this one at Ticklerton to follow the road going south-east to Eaton-under-Heywood.

Local features that indicate drovers' roads:
Pines: SO454900; 466903; 485908; 499928; 461924; 463905; 468908; 506971; 512954

Wenlock Edge, that well-known limestone escarpment, much celebrated in verse, which separates Ape Dale from Corvedale, is criss-crossed by several roads that drovers would have used in their journey eastwards, including commons above Diddlebury, Munslow and Topley. Taking these roads in turn, as we move north-east from Craven Arms, the first two we encounter both ascend the Edge from Ape Dale through Harton Hollow and begin at the T-Junction (SO482880) denoted on the map by the height '176'. The first follows the road to Upper Westhope, and then climbs the track up to Pinstones to descend through Corfton Bache (**Walk 4**), where it crosses Corvedale to join the main drove road that skirts the Clee Hills between Ludlow and Bridgnorth (see Section 2). The second initially ascends through the hollow way opposite the T-junction, then joins the Middlehope road for a short way before dropping down into Corvedale via Dunstan's Lane. It then rejoins the road above Bache Mill before continuing on down and through Diddlebury. Note Little London Farm (SO506885), whose name denotes its historical connection with some old drover who decided to settle here and rest up his well-worn feet.

Continuing north-east along the ridge, the next in line is a route that follows the road mentioned above from Ticklerton. At Eaton-under-Heywood (SO500900) it ascends the edge by the hollow way adjacent to the ancient churchyard. The church has its own magic, flourishing as it does with Green Men and other assorted guardians, while the life-size wooden effigy of some saintly ancient lies reposeful by the altar. On top of the edge the route could either follow what is now the Jack Mytton Way to the road above Black Wood, or drop down through Wetmore Farm and around The Speller to descend into Corvedale via Upper Millichope.

There is possibly another route that leads up from Rushbury onto Roman Bank where it continues a gradual ascent over Topley (SO528905) and then down to Broadstone. And lastly in our sequence, drovers heading north-west towards Much Wenlock are likely to have ascended the Edge at Longville along what is now the B4371 (a road they would have also joined further along if they had followed the route mentioned above that crossed Ape Dale via Hughley).

Local features that indicate drovers' roads:
Pines: SO528905; 543877
Ponds: SO496874; 519854; 506894

Walk 1
The Kerry Ridgeway

Distance: 12 miles
Map: OS Explorer 214

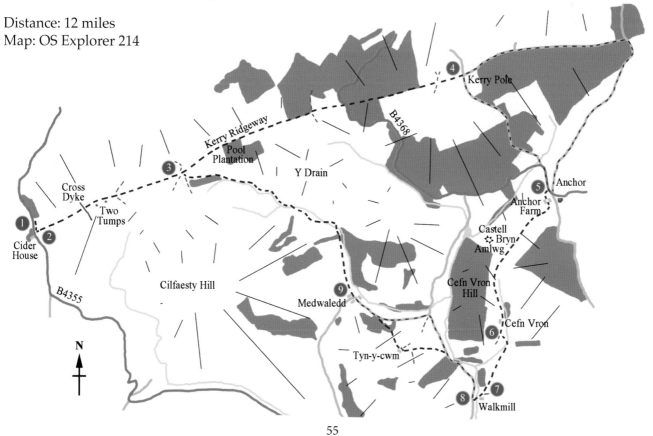

Pool on Crugynnau rise, south of Cider House Farm

The route of the Kerry Ridgeway is well documented and there is a great deal of tourist information about it, including large signs dotted along its route. It never drops below 1,000ft and on a clear day it is said you can see for seventy miles. Its linear nature and height, though, make this famous drove road less amenable to circular walks than most of the others detailed in this book. The fifteen miles of its length can be tackled in a variety of straight sections and from any number of points. You can follow a route walked solely on road, along the five-mile stretch between Pantglas (SJ247896) and Bishop's Castle, or attempt a very full walk that follows its whole length eastwards from where it begins at the Cider House Farm (SO108846), on the B4355 just south of Newtown. Designated parking areas can be found at either end, and also where the B4368 road to Kerry crosses the ridgeway at SO149863, and in Ceri Forest at SO191871. Having said all of this, the walk offered here is a circular affair.

❶ This walk begins at the western end of the ridgeway, in the purpose-built car park situated on the B4355 Knighton-Newtown road, two hundred yards downhill and to the north of **Cider House Farm**. Here, take the designated footpath through the gate and onto the track that ascends through the field by the fence adjacent to the road.

❷ After two hundred yards you will reach a group of trees among which is the residential dwelling converted from the original Cider House on the other side of the road. A signpost directs you sharp left onto a track which follows the line of the fence running up the hill. This is the ridgeway itself, whose 'running fox' emblem is clearly evident on the many signs that direct you along.

Two gates and half a mile later, cross the aptly signed **Cross Dyke**. Ahead of you, over the fence visible on the right, you can see a grassy bump which is the first of the tumuli known as the **Two Tumps**.

Two hundred yards later, as the track levels out, you will arrive at the second tump, which sits on the top of the hill accompanied by a welcome viewing-cairn detailing the surrounding panorama. Visible just beyond the next gate, a signpost points in the direction of Kerry village, lying in the vale below you '6.5 km' to the north. You will begin to see a large group of trees three-quarters of a mile straight ahead of you (known as **Pool Plantation**), in which direction the footpath heads. Before you reach the

The Two Tumps tumuli (rising just above the patch of snow) Kerry Ridgeway

The Two Tumps

As befits such an ancient drove road, the Kerry Ridgeway passes several ancient features and monuments of great antiquity, perhaps the most renowned being the Two Tumps (SO117851), a pair of Bronze Age round barrows that lie close to its western end. There are a larger pair in the nearby village of Kerry, and closer still a cross-dyke one hundred yards to the west. It is said that for a few weeks before and after the summer solstice, the sun can be seen to rise between the 'tumps' from the vantage point of the 'Fowler's Armchair' stone, near Llannano. Continuing east along the Ridgeway the drover would have encountered other cross-dykes and barrows as well as the stone circle at SO158861.

trees, the track dips down to a ford where a footpath rises up to join it from the right. This is the path you will be following on your return journey.

❸ At this point the track continues up along the fence and around to the left of the plantation until it meets the B4368 one and a quarter miles later. To the left, on the other side of the road, you will see the 'Blockwood' designated car-park and another large information board. The Kerry Ridgeway Path (KRP) continues in a direct line straight ahead.

❹ A mile later the KRP crosses a minor road by a house against whose gate sits a sign, **Kerry Pole**. To the left the road drops down to Kerry, and to the right a mile into **Anchor** and the inn that drovers are said to have used.

(Extension: Here our walk heads right towards Anchor, but if you wish, you can extend the walk by going straight ahead. The next mile has some of the most entrancing views to the north and west that the whole ridgeway has to offer. It follows a narrow road that eventually heads through coniferous trees to meet another that also descends to the right into Anchor. Altogether this extension entails an extra two and a half miles of walking.)

If you choose not to extend the walk, simply turn right and walk down the road from Kerry Pole. When you meet the B4368, turn left into Anchor. The famous drovers inn lies at the crossroads on the road signposted 'Beguildy / Knighton'.

❺ Twenty yards before the Anchor Inn, just before the white house on the right, you will come to a signpost by a stile in the hedge. This is where the return footpath begins.

(Alternative: If you would prefer a less muddy and more sure-footed journey back, the alternative is to carry on along the B4368 for the two and a half miles back to where it crosses the KRP at the Blockwood car-park.)

The footpath heads down the slope to a stile in the hedge straight ahead of you. On the other side it takes a sharp left to continue up through the gates of Anchor Farm's yard, beyond which it turns right onto the wide track that runs along the front of the farm. This track, possibly an old drove route in its own right, continues for the next one and a quarter miles to the abandoned **Cefn Vron Farm**. Half a mile along this track you will notice in the valley down to your right the grassed earth and ring-works of the 12th-century **Castell Bryn Amlwg**.

Another quarter of a mile on, the track heads down into a dip where it crosses a cattle grid, the plantation of **Cefn Vron Hill** now rising up to your right. It then makes a gradual ascent to another gate, past which a half mile of descent begins towards a group of firs within which lies the abandoned farm. The track enters the trees and passes a bungalow on the right before crossing the farmyard through a series of gates. It then emerges as the grassy track that continues around the last of the barns and lies above a small valley that drops away to the left.

6 One hundred yards further on you will find a signpost directing you left down towards a stream. However, if the field is very boggy, you might want to continue another hundred yards straight on ahead towards the gate in the fence, before making your descent by the hedge. This brings you down to the stream by a stile; cross the stream by the planked bridge.

The path rising up the other side is hard to discern, but you won't go far wrong if you keep the old gorse to your right-hand side. After 300 yards you will see the roof of a large corrugated barn. Head to the right of this and you will see a stile set in a fence adjacent to a track.

Over the stile, the path continues for another three hundred yards straight across the wildflower meadow that lies before you, towards the corner of the small plantation that rises up from the right.

7 Where it begins to descend you will notice a series of stiles set in the corner where a fence meets the plantation. Continuing to follow the signs, cross these and, bearing just to the right, follow the grassy

Castell Bryn Amlwg

This castle is situated strategically on a hill (bryn) overlooking the Nant Rhydyfedw valley, on an important route to the medieval castle-towns of Clun and Bishop's Castle and at the western edge of the Marcher lordship of Clun established by the Normans in 1070. The grassed earthworks are all that remains of what must have been at its height a substantial and imposing structure. It was enclosed within a stone curtain wall, and had two large D-shaped towers either side of a gateway and a cylindrical keep. There is a notion that part of the structure was built by the Welsh Prince Llywelyn ap Gruffydd during the period of peace that followed the Treaty of Montgomery in 1267.

track that continues the descent alongside an old hedge. Two hundred yards later you will arrive at the bottom where a couple of streams meet by the ruin of **Walkmill**. To your right you will see a wooden bridge and on the other side a stony track; ascend this to the left and follow it for fifty yards, to a minor road.

8 Turn right onto the road and continue for the next one and a half miles all the way to **Medwaledd Farm**. (If you have a map, you will notice a possible short-cut half a mile along this lane in the form of the bridleway that diverts to the left through **Tyn-y-cwm Farm**. However, the locked gate and lack of any signage at either end or in between suggest that it might be better not to use it.) Three-quarters of a mile along the road from Walkmill, a lane to 'Anchor' diverts down to the right. Don't take this, but continue along the road as it bears to the left around the hill for another three-quarters of a mile until you reach the white house and farm buildings of Medwaledd.

9 At this point, leave the road for the track which lies in front of you. This is probably an old drovers' road, one that would originally have carried on over the ridgeway all the way from Kerry. On the left, just before the last hay-barn on the right, stands a large signpost directing the way – 'Fford las 3km'. This is your destination. It is also the point on the KRP mentioned earlier, where the returning path joins it.

Initially the track passes between banked hedgerows, and half a mile later, it descends to a ford which you cross by a wooden bridge. It then doglegs around the large plantation that looms up on the right-hand side, before starting a gradual ascent up onto the open grassland. Veering towards the left, to skirt the flank of **Cilfaesty Hill**, it continues to climb up the small valley that lies between it and **Y Drain Hill** on the right until, a mile later, it finally reaches the ridge and the KRP along which you walked earlier. Turning left here will bring you back to your starting-point at the carpark just below Cider House Farm.

Walk 2
Old Church Stoke to Bromlow Callow

Distance: 4 miles/ 10 miles
Map: OS Explorer 216

Above the much larger Churchstoke, which is situated in the valley alongside the A489, sits its older counterpart, through which drovers would take their animals from the Kerry Ridgeway en route to Shrewsbury. Park in Old Church Stoke.

❶ Follow the road that ascends out of Old Church Stoke to a T-junction at which you bear right towards **Roundton Hill**. After another three hundred yards, you will reach the homestead known as **The Pant Farm** (SJ289950), an apt name considering the climb needed to reach it.

❷ Here, take the narrow walled lane that forks to the left. After half a mile of gradual ascent you will reach **Cowlton Farm**, beyond which the lane becomes the well-defined track that rises

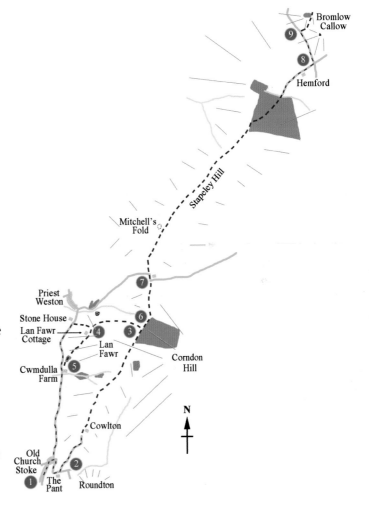

Below the summit of Corndon Hill looking west into Wales

up another half mile to pass between **Lan Fawr** and **Corndon** hills. As you reach the high point of the rise **Stapeley Hill** is visible straight ahead on the horizon, over whose left flank the drovers' road will eventually take you as you continue north and east.

③ Over the rise, as you begin the descent you will notice two footpath signs on your left, fifty yards apart, which point down into a small valley. Take the second of these (SJ301969) to follow the shorter walk.

Shorter walk

The variously marked signpost by a small track that diverts to the left has a sign that reads 'Walking with Offa', and this is the direction you need to follow. It takes you on a descending path through the bracken that skirts the northern flank of Lan Fawr Hill, with the small valley dropping away to your right. As you continue over a stile you will notice the valley of the river Severn opening up before you and, if you are blessed with a clear day, away on the distant horizon the mountains of Wales. These range from left to right: Cader Idris; Aran Fawddy; the Arenigs and the Berwyns.

④ A third of a mile later, after a fairly steep descent, the path reaches a well-established track. Turning down to the right across a cattle-grid, the 'Walking with Offa' path leads down the small lane to **Priest Weston** and its Miners Arms inn. However, you need to take the path signed to the left, which heads up the track to arrive, three hundred yards later, at **Lan Fawr Cottage**.

(Alternative: Just before the cottage there is an easier though less scenic option, involving more road, in the shape of the footpath that is signed to the right. This takes you over a stile into a wild-flower meadow, on the other side of which is another stile in the corner of the hedge signed 'Chirbury Walks'. This brings you into an arable field across which you will see a gate and stile. Turning left onto the lane here will bring you back, one and a quarter miles later, into Old Church Stoke.)

If you choose not to take the alternative route, from Lan Fawr Cottage continue on the footpath and over a stile to follow a fence that runs to the left of the garden. Beyond the end of the fence, continue to follow the path for two hundred yards as it takes you around the side of the hill, before descending down right towards a gate and stile.

The sign here directs you diagonally up the opposite slope of the small dingle to another stile just visible in the hedge. Beyond this, the path continues through the small coppice that lies ahead of you for another two hundred yards, past two benches to a wooden five-bar gate where the trees begin to peter out. Just before this, on your left, you will encounter a stile over a barbed wire fence which you need to cross.

Keep following the footpath, keeping the fence and adjacent hedge to your left. One hundred yards on, towards the end of the hedge, the footpath cuts downhill across the field to another stile which is visible below you to the left. Crossing this stile will bring you out onto the lane just before **Cwmdulla Farm** and the adjacent Willow Bank House.

⑤ Head left along this lane, and another three-quarters of a mile of walking will bring you back to your starting-point.

Longer walk
At the pass between Corndon and Lan Fawr hills, you have the option of a longer walk which, although non-circular, is just as rewarding on the way back as it is on the way out. Having followed the walk to this point (sections 1-3), proceed as follows:

⑥ Continue on down the drovers' track. After half a mile you will come to the road that links the hamlets of Priest Weston and White Grit.

(Alternative: Prior to this point you will pass a footpath sign (at SJ302971) that, if you have the inclination and the legs, will take you on a detour steeply up to the summit of Corndon Hill, from which a grand panorama opens out in all directions.)

⑦ Once you have reached the road, continue along it for fifty yards, past the small parking area on your right, towards the hedged track straight ahead of you. Here a prominent sign for the 'Stone Circle' points in the direction you need. After a quarter of a mile, cross a cattle-grid onto the unfenced moor. From this point on, small signposts denoting a variety of 'ways' (including the 'Stapeley Way' which our walk follows) mark out the path you need. It will take you towards **Mitchell's Fold** stone circle and over Stapeley Hill which lies beyond it.

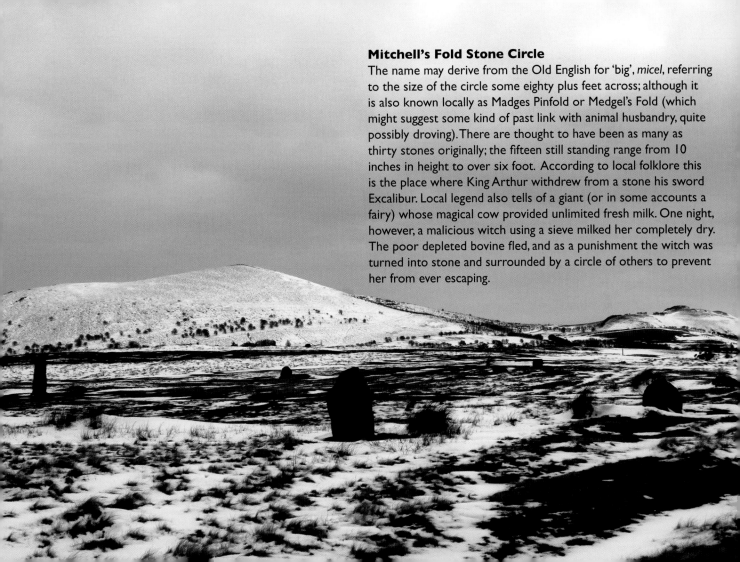

Mitchell's Fold Stone Circle

The name may derive from the Old English for 'big', *micel*, referring to the size of the circle some eighty plus feet across; although it is also known locally as Madges Pinfold or Medgel's Fold (which might suggest some kind of past link with animal husbandry, quite possibly droving). There are thought to have been as many as thirty stones originally; the fifteen still standing range from 10 inches in height to over six foot. According to local folklore this is the place where King Arthur withdrew from a stone his sword Excalibur. Local legend also tells of a giant (or in some accounts a fairy) whose magical cow provided unlimited fresh milk. One night, however, a malicious witch using a sieve milked her completely dry. The poor depleted bovine fled, and as a punishment the witch was turned into stone and surrounded by a circle of others to prevent her from ever escaping.

The initial section of this track shows a very good example of the wide tracks that countless droves over this kind of open terrain have produced. Looking back from the circle you can see the pass between Corndon Hill and Lan Fawr through which you have just come. Further to the right the Kerry Ridgeway is visible and as you continue turning west, there are magnificent views of the Cambrian mountains of Wales stretching out as far as the eye can see.

From the stone circle, continue the gradual ascent over the moorland, and keep following the signposts that skirt the flank of Stapeley Hill which rises on your left, on whose slopes you are likely to see Welsh Black cattle.

(Alternative: A short ascent to the two small cairns clearly visible on its top will afford wonderful views towards the east, in particular the Stiperstones ridge.)

As you round the hill, the pines of **Bromlow Callow** are clearly visible on the horizon straight ahead of you, their promontory rising out of the gorse. At this point the walk starts a quarter-mile descent to the wooden five-bar gate that marks the edge of the open moor. Go through the gate (continuing to follow the 'Stapeley Way' as signposted), and take the fenced track that skirts the left-hand edge of the woodland that lies ahead of you. After 200 yards the track turns right into the trees through which it continues to descend for a third of a mile to the edge of the woodland by a small stream. Crossing this, fifty yards later the track becomes the road which ascends for a third of a mile up past **Hemford Farm** to a crossroads.

8 Here we leave the drove route, which would have followed the road that lies straight ahead via Hope Park Farm towards the A498 and Shrewsbury. Instead, turn left along the road that leads towards the Callow itself, our destination for this walk.

9 After a third of a mile you will reach a 'No Parking' sign on the right. Next to it is a small gate and the footpath sign for the Callow which rises before you. One hundred yards further along the road you will find another footpath through the gorse which is an alternative route up to the Callow.

To return to your start point, simply retrace your steps back to the pass between Corndon and Lan Fawr hills, and either carry straight on the way you came, or take the option detailed in the shorter walk.

Walk 3
The Long Mynd

Distance: 6½/9 miles
Map: OS Explorer 217

Like the Kerry Ridgeway, the Long Mynd offers walks of a variety of lengths along its main drovers' road, the Port Way, but with the added bonus of also having several drove ways that criss-cross it west to east, which increases the options for circular walks. For example, in the Stretton Valley it is possible to climb up to and descend down from the Port Way from a variety of starting points, all of which would have been used by drovers at some time. Moving north along the valley, they begin at the following places, each offering a strenuous half-day's walk:

Minton (SO430908) to Little Stretton (SO440919) – 5½ miles;
Little Stretton to Church Stretton via the Burway road (SO424945) – 6½ miles;
Church Stretton to All Stretton (SO460956) via Cardingmill Valley – 5 miles.

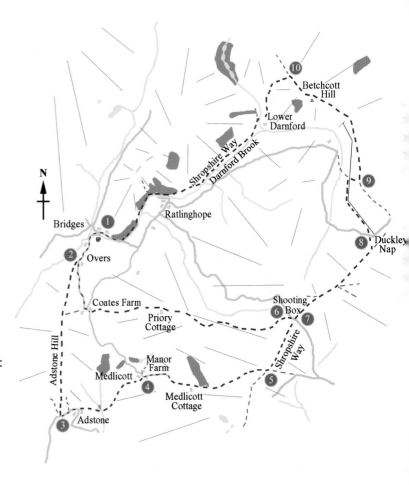

The guided walk I would like to recommend begins on the western side of the Mynd in the hamlet of **Bridges** near Ratlinghope.

1 With the river East Onny on your right and the tables of the Three Bridges Inn on your left, follow the lane that continues up through the tiny hamlet of **Overs**.

The Long Mynd dykes

More than any other period, the Bronze Age has left its mark on the Long Mynd massif – a plethora of tumuli, barrows and several important cross-dykes, including:

Barristers Plain Dyke between Grindle and Round hills. Its main purpose is said to have been to create a barrier to access from the west, cutting off Grindle Hill from the main plateau.

Devils Mouth Dyke between Cardingmill and Townbrook Valleys. It is dated as around 1,500 years old and was probably built to control access along an ancient east-west route followed by the modern day road.

The Iron Age is represented primarily by Bosbury Ring Hill Fort, situated above Cardingmill Valley. It dates from around 500BC and would have faced another hill fort across the Stretton valley on top of Caer Caradoc.

---

2 After a quarter of a mile of gradual ascent you will notice a signpost for the 'Shropshire Way' path (SWP) pointing up the track that diverts to the right. This you now follow for the next one and a quarter miles as it undulates up and over **Adstone Hill**. Initially it takes you through the left of two adjoining five-bar gates and over a series of stiles to the top of the first rise. To your right you will see Linley Hill and the outcrops on the Stiperstones, to the left your destination: the 'hogsback' of the Long Mynd. Just beyond another gate the path joins a track that emerges from your left. This leads down to **Coates Farm**, visible below you, and a lane that descends back to Bridges.

It is also here that a track comes down off the Mynd along which the shorter version of this walk returns. For now though, continue to follow the SWP up over the main top and down through a gate along a hedged section towards another, wider one, beyond which lies a lane on which you turn left. If you were to continue straight ahead, the lane would bring you into Wentnor village whose church tower you may have made out during the descent.

3 Our walk turns at this point towards the Mynd itself. Initially the path follows the lane for two hundred and fifty yards down to **Adstone Farm**, then it leaves the lane to carry straight on through a gate for another two hundred and fifty yards down a hedged track whose signpost is inscribed 'Public Right Of Way'. The track crosses a brook and then rises up the other side for half a mile to **Medlicott**.

❹ Pass to the right of the farm buildings, along with the adjacent **Manor Farm**, and continue up the short lane that lies straight ahead of you, following another signpost.

(Alternative: If you have seen enough ascent today, a return can be made at this point by taking instead the minor road to your left, which will bring you back down, 1½ miles later, to your start point.)

After three hundred yards the lane reaches a gate through which it leaves the trees behind to become the track which snakes a gradual ascent up though moorland onto the top of the Mynd. In the course of the ascent you will reach **Medlicott Cottage** and a gate beyond which you will encounter a National Trust sign informing you that you are now on the Long Mynd proper.

❺ Three-quarters of a mile later, as the track levels out, you will reach a crossroads. Going straight on would bring you to an unfenced road that descends down into Church Stretton, and a detour of some two hundred and fifty yards up to your right would bring you to the Pole Bank trig point, marking the very highest point of the whole massif.

Our walk, though, heads left by the signpost (inscribed 'Boiling Well') onto the SWP again (also signed 'Pole Bank Walk'). This track follows the ancient Port Way route and will be taken across the long top of the Mynd for the next three miles.

After half a mile it descends a slight dip to one of the unfenced roads that cross the Mynd at a parking site known as the **Shooting Box**. At this point you have two options, depending on whether you want to do a short walk or a long one ...

Shorter walk

❻ Turn left here onto the road and then almost immediately leave it for the gravel track that detours from it on the left to head due west. This is unsigned, but represents a very easy to follow 'public access route' that will take you all the way to the aforementioned Coates Farm and thence to the lane down to Bridges. Initially it wends a gradual three-quarters of a mile descent through open moorland until it reaches a fence that emerges from the left. It then ascends for a third of a mile along the fence, over a hill and then for two thirds of a mile down past **Priory Cottage** to Coates Farm.

As the track approaches the buildings, past a solitary pine on the right, you will notice a road-sign to your left – 'Medlicott/Bridges'. Take the arrowed direction for the latter along the road that heads to the right. After it has wound its way between the Farm buildings, it begins a gradual descent past two cattle grids until, three-quarters of a mile later, you find yourself back at your start point in Bridges.

Longer walk

7 At the 'Shooting Box' crossroads, carry straight on over the road following the SWP (including the signposts with a magenta ring near their top). Ten yards on, you will pass a small tumulus on the left, shortly after which the track begins to descend until, a mile later, it reaches another unfenced road.

8 However, three hundred yards before this road is reached you will encounter another track that detours to the left from the SWP, lined initially by eight small wooden stumps. This is a useful short-cut which I would recommend you to take. Like the SWP it too crosses the road, but one hundred yards to the left at a parking site known as **Duckley Nap**.

There is a road-sign here to Ratlinghope and Woolaston, and a footpath sign pointing across the road towards a fence – 'Thresholds'. Take this path, following the fence as it heads over a short rise. The views here are to the north over the Shropshire plain and to the right towards the extinct volcanic hill known as the Wrekin.

The path begins to descend towards the upper end of the Ratlinghope valley. After three hundred yards you will reach a dip and a stile and signpost to your right. Cross the stile and walk for a hundred yards across the field that rises to your right.

9 On the other side of the field you will see another parallel fence by a couple of gates with signs for the SWP. Follow the path as it goes left along the fence in the same direction in which you were originally heading. It now continues for three-quarters of a mile over a short rise, then along by a hedge and up through two gates towards the trig point visible on the top of **Betchcott Hill**. Keeping

THE NATIONAL TRUST

LONG MYND

PLEASE HELP
THE NATIONAL TRUST
TO CARE FOR THIS PROPERTY
BY NOT LEAVING LITTER,
LIGHTING FIRES OR
DAMAGING TREES OR PLANTS
AND KEEPING YOUR DOGS
UNDER CLOSE CONTROL

SEE BY-LAWS ON THE BACK OF THIS NOTICE

Ascending the Long Mynd from Medlicott

Approaching Ratlinghope along the track above the Darnford Brook

this and the subsequent pines to your left, continue along the track through the gate and for four hundred yards down towards another gate in the dip before you.

⑩ On the other side of this gate, set in the hedge on the left by a signpost, you will notice a metal kissing-gate. Here, as the sign informs you, the SWP leaves the Port Way to pass through this gate and bring you back down to Bridges. The route is well-signed and initially wends its way down through open grassland and along the line of a hedge to its left. After six hundred yards it reaches the valley bottom, where it crosses a brook via a couple of plank-bridges and follows a small dyke towards a stile, on the other side of which you will see another stile by a signpost.

Here the 'Darnford Walk' points to the right up along another drovers' track that comes over the hill from Stitt. But you need to head straight on along the SWP down the valley of the **Darnford Brook** which you will keep down to your left. After ¾ of a mile you will reach a ford and footbridge on the outskirts of **Ratlinghope** village. Continuing to follow the signs, cross the stile into the ornamental woodland ahead, in which you will see gardens below on the other side of the brook.

A quarter of a mile later the path comes down to a gate where it crosses a track that heads to the left across another ford. This leads into the western end of the village. Our route, however, continues on over the stile into the coniferous woodland you can see ahead. A quarter of a mile further on the path leaves the trees to cross an open stretch of field before crossing a stile into another woodland, this time a deciduous one. Another quarter of a mile and it reaches a road. Turning right onto this will bring you back, after a similar distance and past the YHA, into the hamlet of Bridges.

'On Wenlock Edge ...' – green lane overlooking Corvedale towards Ludlow

Walk 4
Wenlock Edge

Distance: 6½/10 miles
Map: OS Explorer 217

① Facing out from the entrance to **Diddlebury**
village hall, head towards the right of the church
along the raised pavement in front of it. Where
the pavement ends you will find an overhanging
willow tree to your left and a footpath sign –
'Corvedale/Three Castles Walk' – signs you will
need to follow for the first mile of this walk to
the hamlet of **Corfton**. The first five hundred
yards take you across a footbridge, a stile and
another footbridge until you reach the edge of
the village.

The sign here directs you 100 yards up the
slope of a small field towards a hedge broached
by two successive stiles. On the other side you
need to head diagonally to the right for a quarter
of a mile across a large expanse of grassland
dotted with large oak trees, your destination
being the far corner where a hedge, crossing
from the left, meets a large wood.

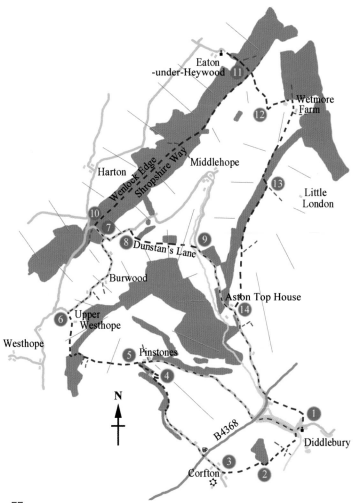

❷ Here, pass through a small steel gate and veer right around the wood, keeping to the right-hand edge of two arable fields. In the corner of the second field, cross a fence onto a track. Turning left, the path directs you immediately to the left over two stiles set in a hedge and into a small field; cross this diagonally right towards the lower end of Corfton.

❸ Here a kissing gate brings you out onto a lane. A slight detour to the left here would bring you to an information board showing you where Corfton's castle used to stand. But to follow our route, turn right and follow the lane for three hundred and fifty yards to reach the main road, the **B4368**. Facing you across the road is the Sun Inn (SO495850), renowned for its home-brewed beers. The route you need lies to the left of the inn, up the lane known as Corfton Bache. After half a mile of ascent you will reach a gate beyond which the lane becomes a hedged track. Follow this, and the track opens out into a green lane which, following the bed of a small dingle, eventually reaches some domestic buildings.

❹ The footpath now dog-legs up the gorse-covered slope that rises to your right, then continues up the dingle at this higher level past the buildings on the left. The path follows a hedge on the other side of which eventually appears **Pinstones Farm**, surrounded by large pines. Where the hedge meets the trees there is a steel gate; pass through this onto a track.

(Alternative: Turning right here would bring you through the farmyard onto Pinstones Lane, which heads back down to Diddlebury, and is an option if it is needed at this early stage.)

❺ Our walk heads left to gradually ascend the blue-arrowed track by the left-hand edge of two large fields, at the top corner of which you will encounter a gate set in the hedge. Beyond this, take a sharp right turn along a path until you reach another gate; pass through this into the mixed woodland beyond. Keeping to the right, this path leads through the trees to the wooden gate on the wood's other side. Through this you descend a delightful green lane that reveals fine views west over Westhope towards the tower known as Flounder's Folly. A quarter of a mile later, pass through a gate onto the track that leads up to the farm on your right (SO477869). However, you continue left, down past the corrugated shed.

6 Fifty yards further on, at a T-junction by **Upper Westhope Farm**'s stone trough entrance, turn right onto a road for **Burwood** and follow it for the next three-quarters of a mile until it merges with one of the roads that traverses the whole width of Wenlock Edge. At this point you have two options, depending on whether you wish to do the longer version of the walk or the shorter one.

Shorter walk

7 Turn right along the road in the direction signposted 'Middlehope/Diddlebury'.

8 A quarter of a mile further on you will come across a hedged track on your right, signed with both blue and red arrows. This short-cut is the old **Dunstan's Lane** (SO487878); take this for the next half a mile as it descends to a gravel track which you join and which then rises up to meet a road.

9 Turning right onto this will bring you, one and a half miles later, back to the main **B4368** Corvedale valley road. In the hedge on the other side of the road, just to the right, you will see a footpath sign pointing through a small gate. Take this path and it

will bring you, a third of a mile, three stiles and the edge of two fields later, through a small gate into the playground of Corvedale CE Primary School.

To your far right you will see Diddlebury church. To reach it and the village hall, cross the playground to the wooden fence. The stile over this leads to a gravel track. Turn right here, through a five-bar gate, and follow the track back to your starting-point.

Longer walk

10 To do the longer version of the walk, at the road junction described in section 6, turn left in the direction signposted 'Eaton Ticklerton' into the woodland. After one hundred and fifty yards you will find a signpost on the left for the 'Shropshire Way'. Join the Way at this point, turning right as directed by the signpost, and follow the signs for the Way for the next one and three quarter miles.

It will initially take you down some steps and across an ancient 'hollow way' that rises up from Ape Dale, the valley that lies beyond the trees to your left. The path then continues straight on along the very edge of the Edge itself, through the woodland and then by the edge of the fields that meet the trees from the right.

After one and a half miles of walking you will notice a modern windmill mast by the roof of the dwelling that lies across the fields to your right. As you pass this mast you will come to a small wooden gate at the far side of the next field.

*(Extension: You could take the footpath down to the left through the trees to the valley below, in which lies the old church of **Eaton-under-Heywood**, which has some of the most renowned carvings of Green Men to be found anywhere in the country.)*

⓫ Passing through this gate, take a sharp right and follow an unsigned footpath for a third of a mile. The path initially runs along the low hedge at 90 degrees to the Shropshire Way path. In the small dale below will become visible the buildings of **Wetmore Farm** (SO508893), your next destination. Beyond them on the horizon looms the large bulk which is Brown Clee Hill.

To reach the farm, the footpath crosses back over the hedge one hundred and fifty yards later via a stile, now signed with a yellow arrow, to descend along the edge of another arable field. Where this low hedge meets another larger one crossing from the right, a stile takes you into a wildflower meadow through which, crossing diagonally right, you will come to an oak tree standing near a lane that runs along the floor of the dale. Reach the lane by crossing over two stiles either side of a fenced brook.

⓬ Turning right here would bring you to the hamlet of Middlehope and the road that leads down to Diddlebury. Our walk though continues left up towards Wetmore Farm and past the old pond on your right. As you approach the buildings you will notice a wide tree-lined green track curving up to the right, rising through fields that lie below the

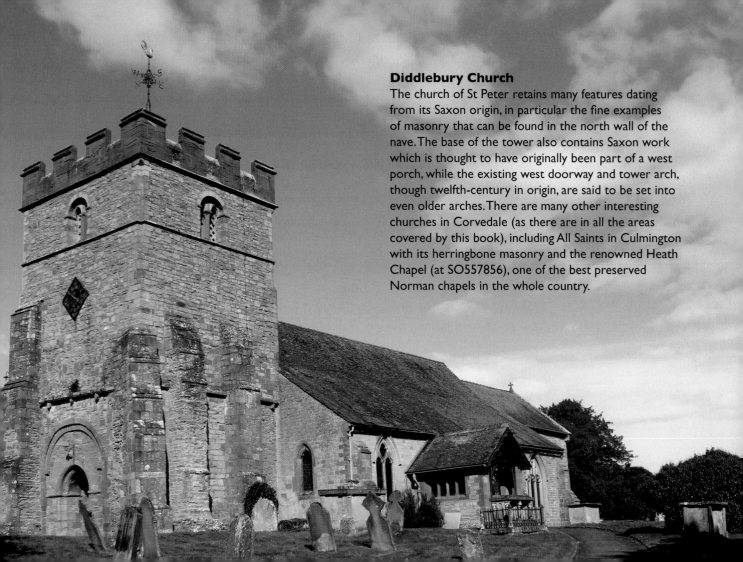

Diddlebury Church

The church of St Peter retains many features dating from its Saxon origin, in particular the fine examples of masonry that can be found in the north wall of the nave. The base of the tower also contains Saxon work which is thought to have originally been part of a west porch, while the existing west doorway and tower arch, though twelfth-century in origin, are said to be set into even older arches. There are many other interesting churches in Corvedale (as there are in all the areas covered by this book), including All Saints in Culmington with its herringbone masonry and the renowned Heath Chapel (at SO557856), one of the best preserved Norman chapels in the whole country.

wooded hillside above. This is the direction you need to take. As you make the gradual ascent that skirts Middlehope Hill you will notice the hamlet nestled in the dale below, and beyond to the west the hills that lie around Craven Arms.

⓭ After half a mile, having passed through two small gates, the path nears the top of the hill and crosses through the woodland. As it emerges to afford fine views east over the Clee Hills, two green lanes will present themselves to you. The one to the left descends straight down towards **Little London Farm**, but you need to take the right-hand fork, which carries on between a hedge and the woodland to your right. The gradual descent of the green lane carries on for a mile, in the distance the town of Ludlow set pleasantly in the valley.

⓮ Eventually the hedged lane, having left the woodland behind, emerges onto the aforementioned road to Diddlebury by the entrance to **Aston Top House** (SO500868). Turning left here will bring you, three-quarters of a mile later, to the B4368.

In the hedge on the other side, just to the right, you will see a footpath sign pointing through a small gate. Go through the gate and follow the path over three stiles and along the edge of two fields, through a small gate into the playground of Corvedale CE Primary School. To your far right you will see Diddlebury church.

To reach it and the village hall, cross the playground to the wooden fence in front of you. The stile over this leads to a gravel track, and turning right here, through a five-bar gate, will bring you back to your starting-point.

Section 2
The Kerry Ridgeway to Knighton and Ludlow

As with the Clun so with the Teme, for its valley is likewise carved in a useful westerly direction, creating a low-level course that drovers may well have followed out of the hills towards Knighton and Ludlow. However, there is evidence of a high-level route that branches from the source of the Kerry Ridgeway at the Cider House, one that traces its way due south and eventually all the way to the town. Initially it follows the B4355 to the pond at SO110840, from which point it continues south across the common's unfenced road to become the footpath that passes south-east between the two tumuli at SO111823. Here it initially follows Glyndwr's Way (GW) before making its long way south-east as the track (**Walk 5**) shown on the OS maps. This meanders around the high ground, crossing Garreg Lywd Hill, Warren Hill and Newhouse Hill, and then heading between Black Mountain and the aptly named Stanky Hill. On reaching the latter it again picks up the GW path and skirts the northern flank of Pool Hill towards the Short Ditch earthwork (SO191748), which is lined with a few score of pines. There is a drove way that diverts just past this point, and heads due east along the footpath that follows the fence over the common land and eventually down into Lloyney. This would no doubt have led to the drovers' inn at Llanfair Waterdine, via Wernygeufron and Goytre Hills. There is also a drove way further back that branches off east (at SO119814), eventually dropping down into Felindre.

The main route to Knighton continues just past Short Ditch along the single-track road and through the gate by a large group of old marker pines that rise above the corner-edge of a much younger forestry plantation. At the T-junction (SO206738) it again picks up the GW path, and follows this all the way to Knighton, apart from the following deviations:

1) At SO211738 the more ancient, though less distinct, drove route heads straight on, following the footpath that rises with the hedge over the hill (marked '375m' on the map) crowned by a handful of pines. Here it joins the single-track road that rises south from Dolyfelin, before heading east to then rise over the hill above the pines at SO220730. At 'Buck Hall' it re-joins the GW path at the gate SO228729.

2) Further on (at the T-junction SO240726) the drove road heads directly across Bailey Hill towards the pines and old quarry at SO246725, rather than dog-legging along the tarmacked road.

3) And finally, just beyond Little Cwm-gilla Farm it may have taken the more direct footpath (SO267724) into Knighton that hugs the southern flank of Garth Hill (although this section would probably only have been wide enough for sheep). There is also the possibility that at the Bailey Hill T-junction mentioned above, a route may have continued along the present-day road over the common where the old Race Course used to be. It would then have made its way down into Knighton on the high-level road that skirts below the mast on the northern flank of Garth Hill.

Local features that indicate drovers' roads:
Pines: SO120825; 123812; 139780; 215737; 248725; 254724; 258725
Ponds: 122809; 209737; 216731; 223728; 225731; 236726; 248725

It might be expected that this very long route south from the Kerry Ridgeway would have been joined and crossed at several points along its length by more localised drove ways, and this seems to have been the case. For example, there is one that ascends from Llanbadarn Fynydd on the road that follows the GW path over Fron Top (SO112790). Turning south the drover could then head towards Knighton or continue east to follow the track that descends through the valley of the Cil-Owen brook into Felindre (see **Walk 5**). Further north at SO119814 there is a diversion that follows the GW up past Bryn-mawr Cottage and down into Felindre. Another route, from Llananno, would have dog-legged east on the minor roads and tracks that go via Drainllwynbir and Little Moelfre farms (SO120756) to ascend the eastern flanks of Moelfre and Gors Lydan hills, before passing over Tynbryniau Hill to join the high-level route towards Knighton.

East of Abbeycwmhir

I have it on the good authority of a local farmer who I encountered in the field one day that two drove routes branch off east from a drovers' road Shirley Toulson identified in her *Drovers' Roads of Wales*, the one which heads north-south along the main road through Abbeycwmhir to meet the A483 just north of Crossgates. The first branch goes to Dolau station via Cwmfaerdy Farm on a track that begins at SO078698, before continuing as the single-track road at SO095690. This then descends to meet the A-road at Llanddewi's bridge, before passing through this village and over Little Hill into Dolau.

The second route branches towards Llanbister, beginning at SO069709 and then heads north-west downhill into the Ithon valley on a track that passes just north of Tyfaenor Farm. It then crosses the Bachell Brook ford before rising through the southern edge of the wood, through the pass and down to 'The Farm' and Llanbister Bridge.

I would like to suggest a third possibility, one that begins at Llidiart y Dwr (SO078716). This route skirts the northern flank of Beddugre Hill to cross the small bridge (complete with pines) over the Ithon at SO100710, before continuing up the footpath to Cefnbronllys Farm (more pines).

From Llanbister there are a variety of tracks that could have been taken by the drover across the extensive areas of commons that stretch east of the village and further south at Maelienydd and Coxhead Bank (**Walk 7**). The route taken, of course, would have depended upon the drover's intended destination, and there appear to be two main candidates. The first is the high-level drovers' road outlined above which runs south from the Kerry Ridgeway to Knighton. This can be accessed at the pass (SO153765) which lies between Newhouse Hill and Stanky Hill, and is reached by the B4356 Llanbister road that heads north from Crossways at SO145741. Further east there is also a track that heads north, at SO185728, up past Dingle Cottage to the marker pines on the hilltop at SO192748.

The second destination, once it was completed, would have been the Llanbister Road Railway Station, where cattle trucks would have been ready to whisk animals away eastwards in a fraction of the time it would have previously taken to walk.

Welsh mountain sheep on Llanbister Common

From Llanbister bridge itself there also seems to be a route that begins on the other side of the A483 at SO103727, where an old track (represented by the present-day footpath) ascends the hill along the southern edge of a narrow copse of pines. At SO107725 it meets the minor road that heads south from Llanbister, which it then continues to follow east via Vronganllwyd Farm to the T-junction at SO144729. At this point the route can either move north to Crossways or continue straight on along the track that meets the minor road at SO172723. Here it has the choice of taking a dog-leg down to the B4386 via Pentwyn Farm or following the footpath that drops down to Llanbister Station by the pond at SO174721.

Another route moves in a more south-easterly direction across Maelienydd and Coxhead Bank commons, following the unfenced road and then diverting south of the minor road from Llanbister bridge at SO124720. It goes past the old Boot and Slipper Inn (SO127717), a venue likely to have been frequented by drovers.

And finally, the road may also have been joined at the ford (SO126723) by a drove way following the track that comes over from Cefn Llanbister from the village, via Llwyn cottage.

The Kerry Ridgeway to Ludlow

From Kerry Pole (at SO164866) on the Kerry Ridgeway another major high-level drove route branches south, before possibly continuing on to Ludlow and beyond into the markets and conurbations of the West Midlands. Initially it passes the Anchor Inn ('drovers still welcome') before heading uphill along the minor road, past an adjacent farm and grazing field, to follow the obvious ridgeway along which the road continues. This goes via Bettws-y-Crwyn (SO207811) and Dowke Hill, to join a south-east track at Stoney Pound (SO239809) which eventually meets Offa's Dyke on top of Llanfair Hill (see **Walk 8**). From here it runs virtually adjacent to the dyke until, at Selley Hall, the route detours up the road (rather than across it) to ascend the eastern brow of Cwm-sanaham Hill. Here the drove way (SO269767) is now some distance from the dyke, whose course at this point is too precipitous for the droving of large herds of animals.

It is likely that tracks would have branched off at Sproad Hill to make use of the drovers' inn at Newcastle and the pasture in the area around Treverward House Farm. Alternatively, for those choosing to head down into the Teme valley to the inn at Llanfair Waterdine, the detour begins at Bettws-y-Crwyn (SO206812). Here the route follows the southerly road that goes via Quabbs and Redgate farms and would have eventually headed all the way west, past Skyborry Farm, into Knighton.

Returning to Cwm-sanaham Hill, the route continues following the main drove way as it ascends the hedged footpath between two now extremely stunted pines (at SO273761), before descending past New House Farm (complete with pines) to the A488 at Five Turnings. There seems to be two possible routes downhill to the main road for our drover. One would go via the remarkable avenue of beech trees (SO274757), past a pond and along the footpath (now unfortunately closed 'by Order'). The other, more likely one, which also avoids the boggy ground adjacent to the stream, would have gone past the farm buildings (at SO274756) and across the fields towards the stand of pines at SO277754, before descending along the track that comes up to join it here from Skyborry Green.

For those drovers whose destination was in Wales and thus had no need to cross the border into England, there are tracks down into Knighton around Panpunton Hill. Stud Farm (SO301731), being close to the town, may have been in its time a place for drovers and their beasts to rest up.

At Five Turnings this route would continue across the main road and along the track that goes over Stow Hill to descend to the bridge over the river Redlake at SO335756 (see **Walk 9**). It would then follow the road into Bucknell (inviting pines at Old Farm) and onto Leintwardine, possibly following the minor road that skirts Coxall Knoll, through Buckton, before joining the main road at Walford ('Welshman's Ford'). Further back, there may also have been a short cut from the top of Stow Hill into Bucknell, down the Cwm and through the plantation, to meet a main track just to the east of Cubbat (SO339734).

Local features that indicate drovers' roads:
Pines: SO1768848; 206812; 221807; 228806; 236811; 242806; 259782; 272768; 272760; 274756; 277752; 282755; 277245; 269742; 355740
Ponds: 179829; 275758

Leintwardine to Ludlow

North-east of Leintwardine (whose old Swan Inn is said to have been frequented by drovers) there appears to be an important crossroads of tracks that meet on the top of Shelderton Hill by the large pine at SO426769. They are reached from the village via the track that goes up past Lower Todding and Mocktree farms. In other directions east and towards Ludlow, the most obvious route for our drover would seem to follow the minor road that runs along the river valley towards Nacklestone and Burrington, where it diverts due east along the footpath (at SO446719) over Bowburnet brow and along the fine green lane into Pipe Aston. At this juncture (SO461721) it joins the tarmacked road from Wigmore, to eventually rise up over Whitcliffe common and down into Ludlow. Drovers heading in the Tenbury Wells direction may have taken the Killhorse Lane (SO456706) over the Goggin to drop down to the Portway at SO489678, before continuing along the present day B4362–A456 road via Tenbury Wells towards Kidderminster.

There also seems to be a variety of higher-level tracks heading east of Leintwardine that would have provided useful panoramas, whilst avoiding the hazards arising from the floods and poor carriageway that closer proximity to the river Teme would seasonally bring. One route may have ascended Church Hill at SO411740 (see **Walk 10**), though the more likely route would have followed the road that branches east of Whitton opposite Dower Cottage (at SO411742). Once on the high ground this would have continued in a north-easterly direction over Downton Common towards Bromfield, while another may have dropped down east to Downton-on-the-Rock (along the present-day footpath that begins at SO420738). There may even have been another following what may represent the old pack-horse route along the track originating half-way up the dingle nestling behind Trippleton Farm (at SO404737), which traces the hill's edge, offering splendid views of the great ox-bow in the Teme's course below. It then dog-legs between the collection of barns above Hollybush Cottage before heading over the field and down through a wooded dingle into Downton Gorge and Bow Bridge.

Having reached the other side of the Teme over the old pack-horse Bow Bridge, the route now leaves the Downton Gorge and rises up through Owney Wood. This area, like much of this medieval Royal

Chase, would have been managed to produce the large quantities of charcoal needed to satisfy the appetite of the Industrial Revolution. Since 1730 it has been part of the Downton Estate, which raises the question as to how accessible this area might have been during various points in its history. However, the ancient track is there for all to see, and at the point where it escapes the Owney trees (at SO447726) it continues in a substantial way heading due east along the ridge. Here it is bordered by an ancient hedge of hawthorn and ash, and from here there is a wonderful view of Burrington Church nestling in the vale below.

After a few hundred yards the route meets at a gate the remnants of two other tracks and merges with the concreted road that rises up out of Burrington. It then continues east over the common toward New House Farm, climbs Bringewood Hill and eventually reaches Ludlow. The area around Burrington Common (complete with ponds) shows all the signs of having been a place where drovers might have been welcomed, and it is well situated for an early start the next day, either to a destination within the town itself or deeper into the Midlands in search of the larger markets beyond (see **Walk 11**).

East of Ludlow

Heading east out of Ludlow towards Birmingham and the Black Country, the drover would immediately have been confronted by those vast, immovable objects known collectively as the Clee Hills. Anybody familiar with their slopes will most likely have been entranced at some time or other by the ancient villages, Norman chapels and Saxon churches that throng this upland area, and the even older stone circles, cairns and green lanes. The A4117 road represents the most direct route due east, via Clee village and the town of Cleobury Mortimer, and its straightness, wide verges and access to common land all suggest that it may very well have been an important drovers' road in its time.

I would like to suggest another route, though, that heads north-east towards Bridgnorth and Wolverhampton, following the ridgeway along which the present Fishmore Road from Ludlow runs, for it seems to exhibit the features we would require in a drove road. To begin with, just out of town there is a toll house (at SO516769), which would only have been situated here if this route had been

The Teme Valley near Leintwardine

used at some time by the drove trade. A little further on, where the road rises, there are marker pines at SO519776 in the woodland above Whitbatch Farm, which also has pines. At SO524799 the road is joined by Thriftwicket Lane, rising up from Corvedale. This may represent a separate drove route heading east in the direction of Hopton Cangeford and The Smithy (SO568817), eventually attaining the pass between the two Clee Hills and thence to Kidderminster via Loughton, Stottesdon and Buttonbridge hamlet.

Back to our Bridgnorth route, there are further pines at a selection of other farms along its stretch: Red Furlongs (SO544827), which was originally known as the Smithy; Cold Weston Cottage (SO552832); Clee St. Margaret village, Abdon and Old Gate farms; and Boundary Gate Farm at SO588876. It is likely that this drove route, if that is what it was, would have been joined in the area once known simply as The Heath (SO555856) by another drove road heading east from Wenlock Edge and Diddlebury via Peaton and Bouldon, before continuing north towards Ditton Priors and the B4368 Bridgnorth road at Monkhopton.

Walk 5
Felindre

Distance: 7½/11 miles
Map: OS Explorer 214

① **Felindre** is a small village
that lies in the Teme valley west
of Knighton. This walk begins at
Upper House Farm (SO168813),
which is situated a hundred
yards along the lane signposted
to 'Llanbister', just off the main
B4355 Knighton-Newtown road.
For the first four miles our walk
follows the well-signed long
distance footpath designated
as **Glyndwr's Way** (GW). This
you will see emblazoned on the
signpost that directs you through
the farmyard and onto the stony
track which clearly ascends
the slope of the hill ahead.
This moves up through open
grassland until, a third of a mile

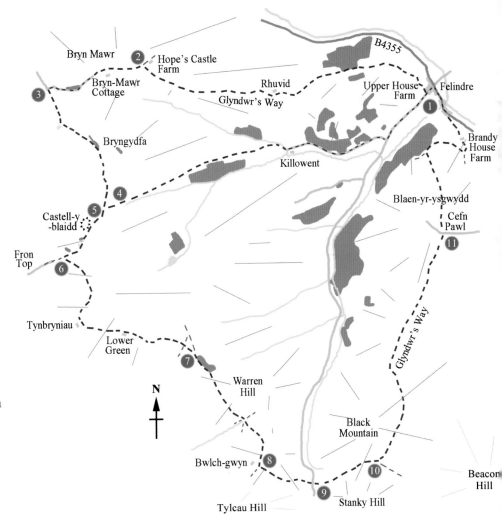

later, it follows the hedge which lies on your right-hand side. At the brow of the hill there are a few pines by an area of woodland on your right.

The track now levels out for half a mile before descending through a five-bar gate and along a hedged track to **Rhuvid Farm**. Continuing through this farmyard past the old pre-fab, the stony track takes you up for a quarter of a mile over Rhuvid Bank and onto open grassland.

Beyond a small coniferous plantation a quarter of a mile further on to your left, you will find the surrounding landscape now opening up in all directions. Up to the left is **Bryngydfa Hill** and its mast, around the other side of which you will soon find yourself. Ahead is **Bryn Mawr Hill** towards which the track now heads. Passing a group of old pines on your right and three more gates you arrive, two thirds of a mile later, at a T-junction.

❷ To your right the track goes to **Hope's Castle Farm**, but you need to turn left onto the track that will shortly become a road. This descends past **Bryn-Mawr Cottage** into the valley. After three-quarters of a mile, where the road veers sharp right, you need to go left as directed by a large signpost and continue to follow the GW path up the hill.

❸ After three-quarters of a mile you will begin to round the western slope of Bryngydfa Hill through a small copse of pines and firs, and a quarter of a mile later you will come to the grassy knoll of the Norman hillfort of **Castell-y-Blaidd**. Here you have a choice between a shorter and a longer walk.

Shorter walk

❹ Instead of continuing on the GW path, turn left onto a well-made stone track which heads eastwards over a cattle grid. After a quarter of a mile the track, which hugs the southern slope of Bryngydfa Hill (you will see the mast on the hill

---

Castell-y-Blaidd Norman hillfort
This horseshoe-shaped landmark – its name translates as 'Wolf's Castle' – is thought not to be the ring-work foundation of a Norman castle, but rather a defensive enclosure, for there are no visible or verifiable remains of building work having taken place here. It measures 35m wide by 55m long, and has a wide entrance that opens at the western end. Sitting high up by a pass where several tracks meet, its strategic position would have afforded superb views of the surrounding area in all directions except the east and north-east.

Castell-y-Blaidd astride the ridge west of Felindre

up on your left), begins to descend a valley with the Trefoel Brook down below to your right. A mile later it arrives at **Killowent Farm**. Here the track becomes a lane which you continue along for three-quarters of a mile, ancient oak woodland rising up the hillside on the left. At the T-junction take a left onto the road which, after three-quarters of a mile, will bring you back into Felindre.

Longer walk

⑤ At this point keep following the GW path, which continues through the dingle that lies ahead of you towards a small group of trees, keeping the hill-fort to your right.

⑥ A quarter of a mile later you will reach an unfenced road which, if you were to turn right along it, would take you over **Fron Top** and down into the Ithon valley and Llanbadarn village. Instead, leave the GW path here and turn left to follow the unfenced road for half a mile down to **Tynbryniau Farm** in the valley bottom below.

Continue along the road which runs left in front of the farmyard towards **Lower Green Farm** a third of a mile further on. Here the road becomes the track you need to follow, which begins on the far side of the farmyard. It ascends the hill that rises in front of you, initially by the fence, and then through open grassland towards the firs that you will see on the horizon half a mile up to your right.

⑦ As you near the trees, the footpath joins a more substantial track coming from the left which it will now keep to for the following mile. Follow it, continuing the gradual ascent and keeping the fenced pines to your left, beyond which the track again enters open grassland. To your right you will see the large massif that is Gors Lydan Hill and, one hundred yards on from the pines, a small sign labelled 'Horse T. Hunt' pointing up to the top of **Warren Hill** (a short detour if you would like to enjoy the panorama looking east over the upper Teme valley towards Llanfair Hill and Offa's Dyke).

Another quarter of a mile on, the track enters a dip, then rises up for another quarter of a mile, past a pond, towards a gate in a fence. At this point the track turns right to follow the fence towards another gate which it passes through. Here, keeping a hedge to its left, it descends for three hundred yards down towards the secluded **Bwlch-gwyn Cottage**.

Arriving from Tylcau Hill en route to Beacon Hill

❽ Here, pass through a wooden gate and turn left to take the unmade road that services the cottage. Follow this for half a mile before eventually descending to a small group of firs where you will find a road. Signs on either side of the road remind you that the land belongs to the 'Crown Estates – Beacon Hill'.

Alternative: To the left the road descends back down into Felindre (which is an option if you decide that you've had enough climbing for the day), to the right towards Llanbister.

❾ Our walk carries straight on, across the road and up the track visible ahead of you. Twenty yards on, it passes through a small wooden gate, then follows the fence on the right. Three-quarters of a mile of gradual ascent will find the track leaving the fence as it rises up to pass between **Stanky Hill** on your right and **Black Mountain** on your left.

❿ Here you once again encounter a sign for the GW path which now rises over Black Mountain all the way back down into Felindre. Take this, leaving the drovers' road that continues over the high ground on its journey to Knighton. The GW path is well signposted from this point and for the next one and a half miles will take you over the long northern flank of **Black Mountain** to descend down to a wall and a couple of gates. Here it joins a track which now rises for a third of a mile through a couple of gates onto **Cefn Pawl** (Pawl Common). By the last of these you will find another 'Crown Estates' sign. In contrast, the commoners' land ahead of you (complete with ponds) would have provided welcome grazing for our drover.

⓫ On top of the common the track comes to an unfenced road, on to which drovers would have taken a sharp right to head down into Beguildy village. The signposts for the GW path however continue across the road, and these are the ones you need to follow. Continue for two hundred yards towards the right-hand corner of the fenced pasture of **Blaen-yr-ysgwydd** straight ahead of you. Rounding this fence, the path gradually descends for half a mile down the northern extent of the common until it reaches a stone track by a fence.

Take this down through **Brandy House** farmyard until, two cattle grids and half a mile later, you arrive back on the main valley road at the edge of Felindre.

Walk 6
Abbeycwmhir

Distance: 10 miles
Map: OS Explorer 214

In her *Drovers' Roads of Wales*, Shirley Toulson identifies a drovers' road that enters this village from the north-west; you will find it just past the house to the left of the church, marked by the large signpost for 'Owain Glyndwr's Way' (GW), which stands by an ancient green petrol-pump. This, she suggests, continues south and east along the present day main road that heads to Crossgates, and it is the start of our walk.

1. Facing the church on the only road that runs through the village, head right along it in an easterly direction past the entrance to the abbey grounds. After two hundred yards, on your left you will pass a large hall set back from the road, known simply as **The Hall**. Down to your right the **ruins of the abbey** itself lie in the vale. Just past the entrance to the hall, take the narrow lane which diverts to the left.

2. After two hundred yards, you will come to a fork in the lane, with a signpost for the GW path directing you along its right-

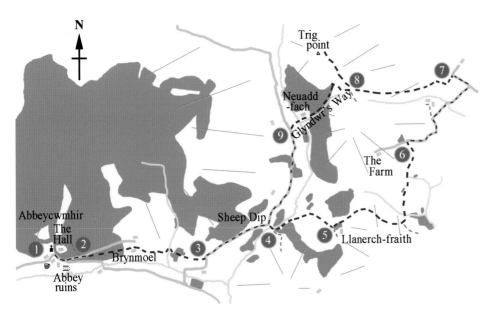

The abbey ruins at Abbeycwmhir

Abbeycwmhir

The 'abbey in the long valley' was built in 1143 by the Cistercians. It would have been the largest in Wales, its 14-bay nave longer than those at the cathedrals of Canterbury, Salisbury and St. David's, but it was never completed. The building was destroyed twice, the first time by the Welsh forces of Owain Glyndwr in 1402, and the second in 1644 by the English during the Civil War. The last native prince of an independent Wales – Llywelyn ap Gruffydd, 'the Last', grandson of Llywelyn the Great – is thought to be buried here. Or most of him at least; his head was removed from his body after he was ambushed and killed at Cilmery, and sent to King Edward I in London. A memorial stone can be found at the site where his remains lie, according to tradition, within the ancient earth of Wales.

hand side. After about half a mile, you will pass the front of **Brynmoel House** and then cross a stream. Rising up from this, walk another quarter of a mile, past a small plantation on your left, then cross a stile into an open field and walk up the steep slope towards another stile in the hedge on the far side. Crossing this, descend a few wooden steps onto a small lane.

3 Turn left along the lane. Half a mile on, it descends though a wood to a small stream (marked on the map as **Sheep Dip**). On your right you will see a white-planked bridge and, just beyond, a steel five-bar gate.

4 Beyond the gate a drovers' road can be seen snaking its way up left through the trees; it eventually rises up through a pass in the hills into the valley of the river Ithon. Considering the inadequate provision of the footpath to the right of this gate (and the one further along the road at SO081720), this track is the most practical route to take.

5 Two more gates and half a mile of ascent later, you will find yourself facing a large stand of Scots pines at a T-junction of tracks. To your right you will see **Llanerch-fraith Farm** with its yard, geese and barns; but you need to turn left, onto the track that gradually ascends around the edge of the hill eastwards through the pass. As you continue along this track, straight ahead, beyond Llanbister village, you will see Beacon Hill and its associates. To your left, on the opposite side of the pass, a white building sits astride another drovers' road – a farm known simply as **The Farm**.

A third of a mile from the stand of pines, the track crosses a very deep cattle-grid by two adjoining gates. Just past this, as the track descends slightly, you will find a gate whose upside-down label, set in the fence to your right, reads 'Presteigne Gates'. Go through the gate and take an unsigned footpath which descends the field to the right of a hedge; it's one hundred yards down to the trees that shelter a small brook.

In the trees you will find a small steel gate through which you pass to ascend for three hundred yards through another field towards a group of firs. Head towards the right-hand corner of these trees where you will find a large wooden shed adjacent to a track. Turn left onto the track, and after another third of a mile, it will bring you to a tarmacked lane which descends to your left from 'The Farm'.

6 Turn right here to head down towards the valley. According to the old maps there used to be a 'pound' nearby. After half a mile the lane reaches a T-junction; turn left to climb back up the hill for two hundred yards.

7 The narrow lane you are on takes a sharp right turn, and you will notice to the left a well-

Llananno Church

The church of St. Anno, which lies a few miles north of Llanbister, between the A483 and the river Ithon, is a hidden gem. Within its Victorian-rebuilt walls stands one of the most finely carved wooden rood screens in the whole area, if not the whole country. It dates to the late 15th century and is said to have been carved by local craftsmen collectively known as the 'Newtown School'. Unusually the screen retains its rood loft, and the whole goes to make an exquisite example of craftsmanship at its very best. Nowhere is this more clearly seen than in the 'knot-tailed wyverns' carved into the large supporting bressummer beam (see illustration below). The church is also blessed with a surviving medieval water stoup and a vestry dated '1681', beautifully carved from an even older warden's pew box. As his poem on the wall suggests, R.S. Thomas often called here. Maybe for you too the screen will lift, revealing something of that 'time older than man' and the 'serene presence' that always awaited his arrival.

established track with a gate at its far end, beyond which stand two tall trees. Take this track for three-quarters of a mile until it finally ascends through open grassland to a col marked by a large GW signpost.

8 Continue straight on to follow the GW path down into the valley below to the road you left earlier, which leads back to Abbeycwmhir.

(Extension: If you have a little to spare left in your legs, a 15 minute detour up towards the right and the **trig point** *on top of Ysgwd-ffordd Hill will present a rewarding panorama in all directions, including Llananno Church nestled by the river Ithon in the valley below.)*

The well-signposted GW descends down the hillside for three hundred yards, then enters a coniferous wood in which it keeps a stream close to its left before arriving, a quarter of a mile later, above **Neuadd-fach House**. Bypassing this to the left, it joins a tarmacked drive which it descends for one hundred yards towards a stream. Here the GW takes a diversion to the right around the small concrete bridge (presumably because of safety fears regarding the adjacent cattle grid).

9 One hundred yards further on you will arrive back onto the road; turn left and retrace your footsteps back past 'Sheep Dip' to your starting-point in Abbeycwmhir.

Walk 7
Llanbister

Distance: 5 miles
Map: OS Explorer 214

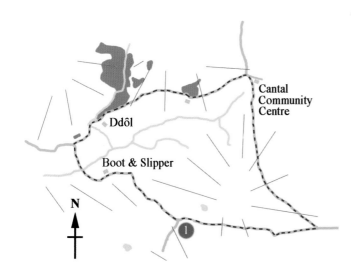

largely unfenced roads that drovers would have used over the Maelienydd commons lying south-east of Llanbister. It also has very few inclines of any particular note, is situated in an area well off the beaten track with very little traffic and, being completely circular, it can be accessed at any point.

❶ I would suggest parking at SO136713, where the road across the common is joined by one coming from the south. From here you can walk along the road west and in a circular direction. After three-quarters of a mile, you will pass the pines to your right that mark the onetime inn still named on the map as the **Boot & Slipper** (SO127717), a place drovers are likely to have frequented.

Continue, heading to the right at each of the three road junctions that you will encounter, and five miles of comparatively easy walking will return you back to your start point.

Alternatively, you may prefer to stroll anti-clockwise along exactly the same circular route, remembering always to bear left at road junctions.

This walk is ideal for those who are less sure-footed and/or insufficiently-booted, for its entire course takes place on the tarmacked surfaces of the

Llanbister Common looking west

Walk 8
Llanfair Hill

Distance: 8 miles
Map: OS 201

This walk follows part of the drovers' road between the Kerry Ridgeway and Knighton along a section where it accompanies Offa's Dyke.

❶ It begins on the western slope of Llanfair Hill at the parking area on the road situated close to a solitary picnic bench (SO249796), beyond which you can clearly see the dyke running across the slope of the hill. The accompanying fenced track that you need to take lies just below it. Turning to look back, on the other side of the road you will clearly see the drovers' road as it arrives from the Kerry Ridgeway, via Bettws-y-Crwyn; this is worthy of a walk in its own right. However, for this walk, follow the **Llanfair Hill** track as it heads to the right and gradually ascends south for three-quarters of a mile towards the trig point which you will see in the field on your right-hand side. One hundred and fifty yards beyond this (at SO256784) the track

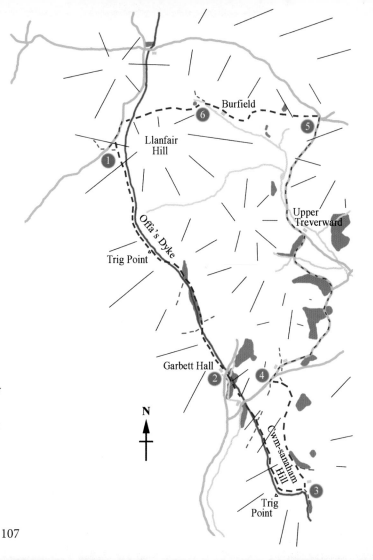

King Offa

The Welsh drovers would have been very familiar with Offa's Dyke and it is more than likely that they would have used sections of it, particularly those in the vicinity of the market towns of Kington and Knighton (whose name in Welsh, 'Tref-y-Clawdd', translates as the 'town on the Dyke'). Today Knighton hosts the 'Offa's Dyke Centre' and the section of dyke just north of the town is one of the best preserved of the whole 177 mile route from sea to shining sea.

Although titled 'King of Mercia' (from 757 to 796AD), Offa could also be described as an early King of England. His kingdom stretched from the Welsh border in the west to East Anglia, and from the Mersey in the north to the Thames in the south. He also had alliances with Wessex and Northumbria through the marriage of his daughters Eadburh and Aelfflaed to their respective kings, Beorhtic and Aethelred.

Offa is also said to have influenced the establishment of the third archbishopric in England at Lichfield Cathedral and to have introduced the 'penny' into English currency. This had the same content of silver as those used in France, making it easier for his kinsmen to trade internationally.

cuts through the dyke and you will now see rising before you a large stand of pines and firs. The track passes through these as it starts a half-mile descent down through a series of gates and gorse into the farmyard of **Garbett Hall Farm** (SO263770).

➋ Cross the farmyard to a narrow road, on the other side of which lies a wooden kissing gate through which the Offa's Dyke Path (ODP) passes to descend some wooden steps towards a stream. Continue to follow the path for the quarter of a mile it takes to skirt a small hill and meet another road.

Carry on straight across following the ODP signs as the path ascends for three-quarters of a mile up to the trig point on top of **Cwm-sanaham Hill**.

➌ Rounding the hill's edge, three hundred and fifty yards later you will arrive at a footpath signed to your left. Here you need to leave the ODP and begin the return journey home north on this path, back over and around the eastern flank of the hill. After a quarter of a mile it becomes the track that will bring you back down to the road you previously crossed.

➍ Turn right. One hundred yards on, you will encounter a fork in the road. Take the left-hand road and continue walking along for the next two miles. The road passes above **Upper Treverward** Farm

Offa's Dyke running south along Llanfair Hill

Offa's Dyke running north along Llanfair Hill

and then begins a long, slow ascent, hugging the hillside to your right, all the way up to a crossroads at SO276800.

5 Here, just before the road forks left to 'Bettws-y-Crwyn', you will find a wide track on your immediate left signposted 'Burfield 1 mile'. Along it also lies the well signed 'Jack Mytton' bridleway. Follow this all the way back for one and three-quarter miles to your start point on the other side of Llanfair Hill. Initially the track will pass through **Burfield** farmyard (and its small wind-generator on the hillside overhead to your right).

6 Through a gate it then continues on the track for 300 yards, before veering left by a solitary oak over a small brook replete with marsh marigolds and cuckoo pint. Here it begins a gradual ascent until two gates and half a mile later the track cuts through a prominent section of the dyke which rises clearly up Llanfair Hill on your left.

Just past this point the gate you need onto the road (at SO251800) is clearly visible two hundred yards ahead. Turning left onto this road will bring you back to the picnic table a quarter of a mile further on.

Walk 9
Chapel Lawn

Distance: 7 miles
Map: OS 201

'Five Turnings' (SO286754), which lies above Knighton on the A488 to Clun, is so called not just because of its junction with the minor road that leads downhill to Chapel Lawn village, but also because of the other set of 'turnings' which represent a continuation of the high-level drovers' road that led south from the Kerry Ridgeway over Llanfair Hill (see Walk 8).

① As you face the white cottage at **Five Turnings** you will see a footpath signed up the wide hedged track to the right of the minor road to Chapel Lawn. This is technically a 'byway open to all traffic', and it is the route you need to take for the next three miles as it gradually ascends up and over **Stow Hill** and down to the river Redlake. Initially it passes through two steel five-bar gates; half a mile later you will come to a third, with the instruction 'Please

Caer Caradoc rising above Chapel Lawn

Shut', after which the track follows a single, smaller hedgerow laid to your left. Visible, half a mile ahead of you, is a large coniferous plantation with a wide gap through which the track continues.

(Extension: Before reaching the plantation, a detour up through the grassland to the brow of the hill on your right will afford fine views overlooking Knighton and, further on, the mountains that rise behind Radnor, Hay and Brecon. In the opposite direction, east, you will see two 'Caer Caradocs': one immediately in front of you by Chapel Lawn; the other to its right on the horizon, near Church Stretton.)

2 Reaching the edge of the plantation, the track continues for two thirds of a mile straight along the edge of the trees.

*(Extension: Another worthy detour can be taken on the footpath that carries on up the hill to your right through the middle of the field. This heads past an old pond to your left and around the corner of the smaller plantation that sits on the hilltop. Two hundred and fifty yards ahead of you is the trig point at the top of **Stow Hill**, which provides glorious views in all directions. Below, you can see the track to which you need to retrace your steps.)*

3 At the corner of the large plantation, rather than descending down the forestry track that turns to your left by the trees, carry straight on along the footpath that continues on through the double gates. This section of the wide track has a fence to your left and the open field rising up to your right.

4 A quarter of a mile further on you will arrive at a crossroads of tracks near the corner of another plantation. Here, take the footpath signposted to your left which continues along the byway as it descends down into the **Redlake valley**. It goes through the gate visible ahead and past the small group of firs on the left. As you descend you will be able to see more clearly around to your left the western flank of **Caer Caradoc** hill, with Chapel Lawn village at its base.

The track continues for half a mile through more gates and eventually to the right of **Vron** farmyard, after which point it becomes hedged on both sides. Close to the bottom of the descent, a quarter of a mile later, the old way through **Lower Lye**'s farmyard has recently been replaced by a diversion which goes to the right above the farm, then re-joins the original track and crosses a small bridge over the river to reach the road in the valley bottom.

Between Vron Farm and the river Redlake

5 Turn left and simply continue along the road for one and a quarter miles to **Chapel Lawn**.

6 A quarter of a mile beyond the village a small lane diverts to your left signed 'Five Turnings'. Take this as it wends its way up around the northern flank of Caer Caradoc, noting the pines as you go. It will eventually bring you back, after one and three-quarter miles of ascent, to your starting point at Five Turnings.

Walk 10
Leintwardine

Distance: 9 miles
Map: OS Explorer 203

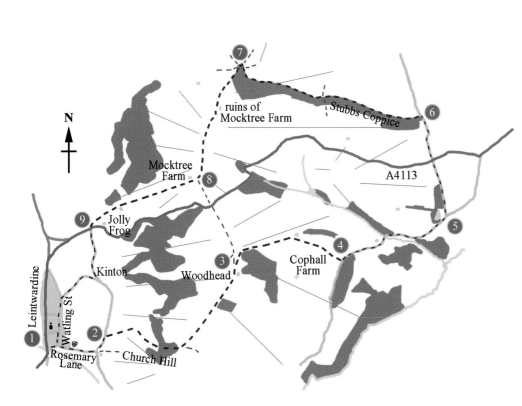

N

ruins of
Mocktree Farm

Stubbs Coppice

Mocktree
Farm

A4113

Jolly
Frog

Cophall
Farm

Kinton

Woodhead

Leintwardine

Watling St

Rosemary
Lane

Church Hill

① With the village green at your back, turn right away from the bridge and walk for three hundred yards along **Rosemary Lane**, which begins at the bottom of **Watling Street**, and past the old Sun Inn ('of well-deserved fame') towards the base of **Church Hill**, which rises in front of you. Here, at a T-junction, instead of taking the steep footpath that lies beyond the small metal gate, take the road to your left, signposted towards **Kinton**.

② Two hundred yards on, just before the road rises by the small wetland (where ragged robin grows in June), you will see a track that begins at the gate/stile on your right-hand side (SO411740). This ascends more gradually for three hundred yards up to the top of Church Hill.

Pass through another small metal gate in the corner of the field where a large hedge begins, then continue along this track for a mile in a north-easterly direction to what was once **Woodhead Farm** (SO425746), now subdivided into a series of smaller properties.

③ At this point, take the footpath signed to your right, just past the farm, and head diagonally right across the field. After three hundred yards you will reach a dirt road. Turn right onto this and follow it down over Downton Common, passing the large farm buildings of **Cophall Farm**, until you eventually come to a road.

④ Here, turn left to pass a series of estate dwellings until, just past a large sign to Downton, you reach a fork in the road.

⑤ Take the left fork and continue along this road for a third of a mile and across the busy **A4113**

until you descend, a quarter of a mile later, a slight wooded dip.

⑥ As the road begins to rise you will notice an especially large oak on your right and, just beyond this, a signpost for the 'Herefordshire Trail' pointing up to a track on your left. This you take for the next one and a quarter miles as it gradually ascends the hill, keeping the bluebells of **Stubbs Coppice** sloping down to your left. The coppice eventually becomes a fir plantation at the end of which you will notice a large pine on the other side of the track, standing alone near the junction of several other tracks. The wonderful views here take in a panorama that reaches anti-clockwise all the way from Ludlow around to the Clee Hills, the whole of Wenlock Edge and, to the north, the Stretton Hills in the distance.

⑦ Here you need to take a sharp left onto the grassed track that skirts the western flank of the plantation whose northern side you have just ascended. A quarter of a mile later it becomes a stony, potholed road. Two hundred yards further on, this passes to the right of the **ruins of Mocktree Farm** to reach, and half a mile later, you will come

Moving east of Leintwardine above Whitton

to another **Mocktree Farm** that is still very much in one piece.

⑧ At this point, instead of taking the road to your left that drops down to the A4113, follow the bridleway signposted straight ahead of you along the hedged track towards Mocktree Cottage (also with its own dilapidated predecessor). Descending down three-quarters of a mile into the Teme valley this track, which becomes tarmacked at the Todding, eventually reaches the A4113 above Leintwardine.

⑨ Here, instead of turning right onto the busy main road, it is much more pleasant (and undoubtedly safer) to take the lane immediately opposite that takes you down for a third of a mile into Kinton hamlet. When you reach the T-junction, turn right and walk back into Leintwardine, a quarter of a mile later, where the lane joins Watling Street by Dark Lane. Turning left here will bring you past the school and cemetery back down to your starting point at the village green.

Walk 11
Burrington

Distance: 6 miles
Map: OS 203

1 Begin the walk at the
church. With your back to it,
turn left along the village's
only road towards **Burrington
Farm** and the hill that lies
beyond it. Just past the farm
you will find a concrete track
that ascends to the left. Twenty
yards on, where it takes a
sharp right, you will notice
an old track joining it from
the left, rising up from Bow
Bridge over which packhorses
are said to have crossed the
Teme in Downton Gorge.

Continue right along the road for three-quarters
of a mile to **New House**, which is surrounded by
very large pines, but may be too recent a property to
have been used by the droving trade.

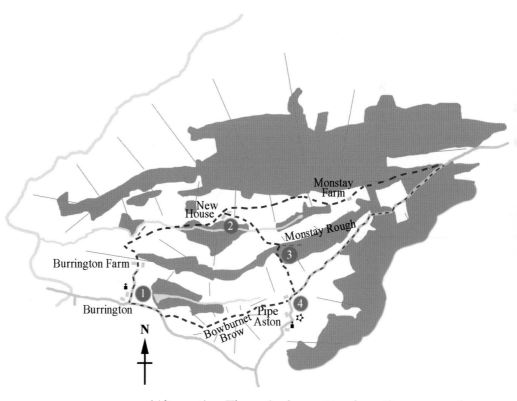

*(Alternative: The main drovers' track continues around
to the left of the house along which a signed footpath rises
up to eventually skirt the southern flank of Bringewood
forest. After one and three-quarter miles it gradually
descends down to the main road (SO479736).)*

119

At this point turning left would bring you to Ludlow and right back towards your start point. This latter route could be taken, but bear in mind that it will entail either a return journey of 1½ miles by this busy road to Pipe Aston, or retracing one's steps back to New House.)

② To follow our walk, though, take the signed footpath to the right of New House which begins between the house and the new-build to the right. Passing through the wooden five-bar gate, follow the footpath keeping a low hedge to your right for one hundred yards. Then continue through another gate for another hundred yards.

At this point follow the path as it detours through a gate set in the hedge, down into the small wooded dingle below. Passing through the dingle you will soon cross a small stream, heading towards the old metal gate ahead (complete with blue bridleway arrows). Ahead of you the path keeps to the left of a hedge and then, just beyond the copse's last trees, it climbs slightly to the left and up through a field for three hundred yards towards a couple of gates now visible at the base of the fir trees on the skyline above.

Pass through the gates into the plantation of **Monstay Rough** which descends into the valley below. The path you need takes a very short right, before descending twenty yards steeply to the track visible below.

③ Follow the footpath sign directly in front of you and take a tricky, though short, descent of some two hundred yards down to a stile at the edge of the wood. Here there are fine views west towards Leinthall Starkes and Wigmore. Crossing into the field, continue downhill for one hundred and fifty yards to the old five-bar metal gate in the hedge at the bottom. Go through this, and walk three hundred yards across another field to a gate (and stile) on the other side of which is the road and village.

④ Turning right here, pass Halfway House ('halfway' to Ludlow perhaps, but from where?) immediately on your left. (You may see the resident geese and ducks.) Straight ahead of you, at the bend in the road, is a hedged green lane. Take this, and walk the mile-long short-cut of an old road that originally passed over **Bowburnet Brow** from Burrington, though today only the section now facing you remains.

As you walk along the signed footpath, a third of a mile further on you will approach the top.

Bowburnet (the slope in the middle distance) from Bringewood, above Pipe Aston

Burrington Church's cast iron grave slabs
Alongside the outer wall at the east end of the church of St. George lie an unusual group of eight grave slabs all cast in iron between 1619 and 1754. They were produced at a nearby foundry, located in Downton Gorge, and using charcoal produced by the wood burners who worked in the surrounding forests of Bringewood. One of the slabs commemorates Richard Knight (d. 1645) whose family of noted 'iron-masters' owned the foundry and are thought to be responsible for similar slabs to be found in the church of St. Leonard in Bridgnorth.

Here the hedge runs out and the path swings to the right to continue along a fence now to your left. Ahead of you the very top is crowned by a concrete water tank contained in a small enclosure. Past this point the path gradually descends straight and to the right of another hedge until half a mile, five stiles and a couple of fields later you reach a road.

Turning right along this for a quarter of a mile and then right again will bring you down to your start point in Burrington village.

Section 3
East of Kington and Hay

Presteigne

Though smaller than its neighbours Knighton and Kington, Presteigne was as important a town as any in the area and it seems likely that it would have encountered its own share of the droving trade. However, I have yet to discover records of such, though the present-day B4362 road that heads east via Shobdon may represent a major drove route. Another candidate may be the track that initially follows this road to divert north-east towards Lingen, just north of Kinsham, where it follows the hedged track that begins at SO368654. This descends down to the ford at Lower Yeld and thence along the lane to Upper Lye, before continuing east along the road through Lower Lye. Just past Ballsgate Common it diverts onto a track that goes up over the pass to round the northern slope of Pyon Wood hill, before crossing over the A4110, through Yatton and up onto the heights of Croft Ambrey. Here extensive grazing and springs would have been available on Bircher and Hanway commons, while the whole area offers numerous ancient ways (including Welshman's Lane and Green Lane) that stream down its eastern slopes, any one of which may have been favoured by our drover.

There may be another route from Presteigne that joins this one at Lower Lye. To find it, from the town centre take the road that heads past the church and up the hill around the western reaches of Stapleton Castle towards Lingen. The direct route down into the village may have turned right at SO333664, to follow the ridge of Stapleton Hill along the track that goes through New House Farm. (There might even have been another way that headed downwards in a more southerly direction towards Limebrook Priory (SO374661), where an ascent past the mill, on the wide track that skirts the wood, eventually joins up with

Looking south from Bringsty Common

the main route.) Carrying on from Lingen, the most likely route follows the road which ascends towards Deerfold, to eventually head east to Ludlow via Wigmore and Leinthall Starkes. Likewise, a route in the direction of Tenbury Wells may have diverted from this at SO372671, taking a left along the track that climbs up above Deepmoor Farm to a crossroads of sorts at SO384670. At this point it would have followed the road towards Lower Lye that joins the route outlined in the previous paragraph.

Local features that indicate drovers' roads:
Pines: SO328661; 345664; 366671; 417664; 426666; 439669; 461676
Ponds: SO461676

Kington

According to Shirley Toulson, drovers heading east out of the mountains and valleys of mid Wales channelled into three main drove routes as they converged on the area around Llandrindod and Builth Wells. The first, and most southerly, moves from Builth through Cregrina, Rhulen and Newchurch, to meet the banks of the Wye at Rhydspence. The other two converge on Kington. The one heading from Llandridod and Pen-y-Bont diverts from the A44 by that renowned drovers' hostelry the Fforest Inn (SO171585), where it continues over the Cefn Perfa through Yardro and Dolyhir, before again picking up the A44 road at Stanner; the other arrives over Hergest Ridge from Newbridge-on-Wye via Glascwm and Gladestry (see **Walk 14**). According to local Kingtonians, drovers also passed through Barton Farm, to the north-east of the town centre, perhaps as a way of avoiding its tollgates.

Continuing east from Kington, evidence on the ground and in the archives peters out, short of the vague notion that the drove road simply followed the A44 all the way to the Bromyard Downs via Leominster. From here the route would have continued along the A44 towards Worcester, via the grazing offered on Bringsty Common and then, more than likely, all the way to Oxford, following the occasional marker pines that can be found en route. Drovers may also have diverted south from Bromyard to Ledbury and Malvern, along what are now the present day B4214 and B4220 roads respectively. Bromyard's famous downs (see

Walk 16) are said to have provided grazing and ponds for beasts, while for the drovers themselves the Royal Oak inn provided a well-reputed, welcoming watering-hole.

Returning to the A44 at Kington, there are very few references to anything of a droving nature between here and Bromyard, apart from two anomalies that have puzzled me greatly, for both seem somewhat askew of this route. One concerns the Stagg Inn at Titley (SO329598), which lies north of the A44 and prides itself on being at the convergence of 'two drovers' roads'. The other is that presented by the Drovers Barn near Broxwood, some way south (SO378545): self-catering accommodation that also advertises its past droving credentials. It was only when I went out into the field and started becoming familiar with the physical topography of the landscape that the fuller story began to reveal itself. Not only are these two places possibly connected; they also reveal the wider necessity for drove routes heading south and east from Presteigne and the area known as the Walton Basin that lies between Knighton and Kington.

Yet again, a high-level, ancient ridgeway seems to play its part in our drovers' story – in this case the one that follows the green lane that runs above Titley along the present-day Mortimer Trail from Green Lane Farm (SO323614) to the top of Rushock Hill (SO289596). As is to be expected, there are several places from which this route and its commons can be accessed, depending on the particular lowland pasture from which the animals originated and the destination that was to be their fate.

For example, if the drover came from Presteigne east around the inaccessible and densely wooded massif that stretches from Nash Wood to Burfa Bank, the old lane that rises up from Rodd Hurst (SO326621) may have been used. If, however, he was to come around from the west (and also wanted to avoid the turnpike at SO273601) then the Offa's Dyke path that rises up from Lower Harpton ford could have been the preferred choice. There may even have been a route halfway between the two, rising up from Nash (see **Walk 13**). Conversely, drovers heading in the direction of Ludlow via Presteigne, might have used the Rodd Hurst route in the opposite direction.

There seems to be a plethora of old tracks and hollow ways that would eventually lead to Lower Harpton and Presteigne from across the Walton Basin and out of the outlying villages, hills and valleys that range east of the hills of Radnor Forest. They include, just south of Cascob (at SO237656), an enchanting

Green lane above Titley

Green lane above Titley

'crossroads' of green lanes situated on a drovers' road which the farmer at nearby Newhouse Farm suggests rose over the hills heading east from Bleddfa, down the old Ackwood Lane to Beggar's Bush and beyond. The Red Lion at New Radnor is said to have been a drovers' inn, while the Offa's Dyke path south of Evenjobb seems substantial enough to have possibly been used for droving at some time in its history.

There is another likely route which heads south of Discoed (SO277649), past Thorn and over Evenjobb hill to cross the Slough Road at Sunnybank, before dropping down via Darbank Farm to the dyke at Burfa (SO279615). Here the old, high-level county road (noted by R. Colyer) was probably used by those drovers whose business led them east of Evenjobb towards Presteigne and beyond towards Ludlow (see section 2), rather than south to the A44.

Local features that indicate drovers' roads:
Pines: SO276630; 281621; 281633; 289633; 272620; 439575.
Ponds: SO279622; 319612

Back to Rushock Hill, and continuing south along the Offa's Dyke Path, this route would bring our drover down to the inns and shoeing stations of Kington, and thence east onto the A44. Alternatively, at the eastern end of the Green Lane ridge previously mentioned, a pre-enclosure way down to Titley probably followed the present-day Mortimer Trail over the crest of the hill (at SO326612) and down to the church. Another option may have been the road that drops down from Green Lane Farm to arrive at the Stagg Inn. There may very well have been a third route down to Titley from Burnt House (SO314610), a route which meets this road at Turning Ways Farm (SO326603). From Titley there seems to be evidence for a minor route following the lane that leaves the B4355 at SO333602 and heads past Priory Leasow towards the pines above The Forge (SO348591). From there it would head south-east via Marston and Weston towards the Drovers' Barn to the east of Lower Broxwood, before eventually meeting the A4112 below Little Sarnesfield. From here the route would have gone through Weobley and along the road that goes south to Hereford via Wormsley and Tillington Common. Evidence of pines north of Little Sarnesfield suggests that it might also have been connected by another drove route, this time from Kington via Lyonshall. Pines can be found along the minor road that leaves the A480 at Woonton Ash (SO 348543), and heads through Bonds Green and Passey Grove. The A480 may itself represent an old drove road to Hereford.

Local features that indicate drovers' roads:
Pines: SO348591; 357586; 375547; 383532; 385522; 316562; 340551; 350545; 355545; 361540; 366535; 444542
Ponds: SO384529; 348542; 365537; 364528

Rhydspence to Hereford

The Rhydspence Inn near Hay-on-Wye (see boxed text in **Walk 15**) features in virtually every book and guide written to date about the Welsh drovers, and is perhaps the best extant example in the area (if not the whole country) of a recognised drovers' inn which incorporated what has been termed a 'shoeing station'. Not only did it accommodate and refresh both drovers and beasts after their long walk over the Welsh hills (it still retains a 'Drovers' Barn' renovated for today's footsore traveller); it also had a smithy that provided the variety and type of shoe that different animals would have needed to cope with the harder surfaces of England's metalled roads. Painscastle had a similar set-up at the Maesllwch Arms, as did Kington and Whitney, whose drovers' inn and smithy are now private dwellings. The New Inn at Brilley is also said to have accommodated drovers in its time.

The route from the Rhydspence stays north of the river and heads due east to Hereford, via Willersley, along the A438. It may be the case that a diversion was taken along the course of the older Roman road that leaves it just past the Portway (at SO385441). If so, this would have taken the drover north of the city centre and brought him to what would have been a large natural holding-pen in the shape of the extensive meadows to the east of the river Lugg (SO535417). There is an old trackway here that may have been used to access them, near the two pines that identify where the old Roman road leaves the younger A4103 (at SO539418). There are several other old pines along this route from Willersley, as well as some ponds near the remains of the old Roman town originally known as *Magnis* (SO442427). The farm here may also have supplied board, along with those at Barnfields and the one by the church in Staunton-on-Wye. We should also note Little London Farm north of Staunton (SO359460).

In *The Drovers* (Shire Publications), Shirley Toulson outlines a detour from the route into Hereford that drovers took to avoid the toll at Portway. It lies between the old Roman road (A438) and the river Wye and follows the present-day Wye Valley Walk as it heads east of Bredwardine from The Scar (SO351445) along 'Monnington Walk', before joining the A438 between Byford and Bridge Sollers.

Local features that indicate drovers' roads:
Pines: SO410433; 458425; 467429; 418539
Ponds: SO434426

Hay to Hereford

Back in Wales, there are no doubt extremely old drove roads running south of the market towns of Brecon and Hay-on-Wye that would have traced the numerous ridges along the high Beacons and Black Mountain ranges. It is quite likely that the lower ridges running south-east from Hay along the higher ground between the Black Mountains and the Golden Valley would have been used by drovers – for example, the tracks that skirt either side of the Black Hill (SO275348) via the Olchon valley and Craswall respectively, and the routes that rise over Cefn Hill to follow the old Cefn Road (SO287366); and further east, the routes over Vagar Hill (SO291393) and Urishay Common (SO312371).

Meanwhile, drovers heading towards Hereford could avoid the toll bridge at Whitney and the tollgates near Hardwicke and Bredwardine (whose adjacent tollhouse can still be found on the present day B4352 at SO331447), by following what is today designated the Wye Valley Walk (WVW). According to Shirley Toulson, the drovers' route leaves the B4352 by the pub at SO291452 to climb up to the top of Merbach Hill (see **Walk 15**), where it splits from the WVW just past the trig point (at SO305447). At this point it drops down the bridleway to join the narrow lane at the 254m height mark, before continuing downhill to the bridge at Bredwardine. This route would have allowed access to the good pasture to be found on the hill's

Between Merbach and Bredwardine hills

extensive common land. Drovers may also have descended the southern flank of the hill into Dorstone and the Golden Valley along the tracks that descend from Arthur's Stone Lane (SO317432).

Local features that indicate drovers' roads:
Pines: SO414551; 415553; 416556; 421565; 427593

Hereford to Worcester

After resting the night in the environs of Hereford there are two 'ancient track-ways', briefly sketched by K.J. Bonser in *The Drovers*, that eventually lead all the way to London. One heads in a westerly direction via Ledbury, Little Malvern, Bredon Hill, Broadway, Banbury and St. Albans. The other moves south-west through Newent and Gloucester and then either via Cirencester and the Ridgeway at Uffington, or via Abingdon and the Chilterns at High Wycombe.

I would like to suggest possible evidence for a third route, one that would have continued along the Roman road that runs north of Hereford (mentioned above). It is shown on the OS map joining the present-day A4103 at Shucknall before heading north-west to Worcester. If the Lugg meadows were used, the obvious way for the drover to rejoin the course of the Roman road would have been to retrace his steps back to where it leaves the A4103 by the two pines previously mentioned (at SO539418). However, there is some evidence of a short cut that takes the ridge that runs west along the high-ground of Hemhill towards Wilcroft (SO565417). This is accessed by continuing along the track that runs across the meadows towards the public footpath beginning at SO414556, which then rises up through the northern edge of Lugwardine to attain the brow of the hill above Prospect Cottage (SO414551). This point is marked by a clump of eight marker pines that are clearly visible from the meadows to the west. There are more old pines along this route that might indicate the further direction of a drove route, and another clump that can be reached either by passing through the hamlet of Wilcroft and then following the road north, or by taking the public footpath downhill which meets the Roman road at SO420562. Further on there are a large group of pines at SO427593, where the A4103 reaches a high point as it skirts the southern slope of Shucknall Hill.

Hollow way between Bleddfa and Cascob

Walk 12
Cascob

Distance: 5 miles / 5 miles
Map: OS Explorer 201

These two walks traverse the area between Presteigne, Kington and the hills of Radnor Forest, taking in drove roads, green lanes, turnpikes and, for good measure, sections of Offa's Dyke. The walks could be enjoyed on different days, or attempted on one day, interspersed, perhaps, by a lunch-break in the churchyard.

First option

① Just before the road that rises up to Cascob Church crosses a bridge, a lane diverts off to the left along which a bridleway is signed 'Powis'. Follow this for the quarter mile it takes to makes a gradual ascent up to a cream-coloured cottage. It then continues as the green lane that lies to the left of the cottage for a further seven hundred yards until it meets a gate, beyond which it enters a field to the left of **Ack Wood** plantation. On the other side of the field you will find another gate that leads onto a crossroads of green lanes (SO237656).

Track south of Forest Wood between Bleddfa and Cascob

② Straight ahead, the lane you have been following continues down to **Ednol Farm**. You will eventually make your return along this lane, but for now, make a left turn and head up the hedged track known as 'Ackwood Lane'. This old drovers' road follows the ridge of the hill before eventually descending down to Beggar's Bush and thence to Presteigne and beyond. Follow it for three-quarters of a mile as it gradually ascends east and then follows the contours of the hill south.

③ At the point at which the track reaches a plantation and bends left alongside it, you will find a gate on your right through which begins the hedged bridleway that you need to take. One hundred and fifty yards on, another gate leads into the yard of an area known as **New Buildings**. Turn right here towards a gate on the other side of the yard through which lies a field and a large hedge. The blue arrow on the signpost by the gate points in the direction you need to take – a bridleway that continues along the track by the side of the hedge.

This continues for a third of a mile along the brow of the hill, through another three gates and fields, until it makes a gradual descent towards a fence/hedge. Here you will find the aforementioned green lane that rises up from the road by **Ednol Farm** and a steel gate on your right through which the walk proceeds. This goes back up for a quarter of a mile to the green lane crossroads. At this point, continuing straight on, walk another half a mile back down to the bridge below Cascob.

Second option

From the bridge at Cascob walk up the road, past the church on your left, and carry on for half mile until you reach **Twiscob Farm** (SO231660) and its scattered array of outbuildings.

④ Just beyond a half-built breeze-block structure, a signpost points up the hedged track that rises to your right, and this is the track you need to take. (If you were to continue another two hundred yards along the road, you would find the continuation of the drovers' road that heads down this track descending to your left. This eventually fords the brook and rises up the hill via Newhouse Farm to meet the green lanes featured in the walk above. But at the time of writing the path is so overgrown as to be impassible.)

After a third of a mile of ascent the track reaches the brow of the hill and begins to level out. Behind you the views stretch south-east as far as the Malverns on the distant horizon. Here the track is joined by another from the left, at which point, continue right towards the corner of the plantation known as **Cascob Firs**, along whose edge the route now continues towards an even larger plantation called **Forest Wood**. Another third of a mile and you arrive at a more substantial T-junction (SO228668).

(Alternative: The tarmacked road to the right descends for a mile down to your start-point at the bridge, and this is an option if you feel enough has already been achieved for the day.)

⑤ The route to the left extends this walk by another three miles and does involve some fairly steep sections of ascent and descent. Initially it follows a blue arrowed bridleway for half a mile through a gate into the field beyond, parallel with the line of trees on the right and toward the right-hand corner of the large plantation that looms on the horizon.

Two gates later it arrives, where the field ends, at a third gate through which the bridleway continues straight on across a forestry road. At this point it descends a green track with a hedge and felled plantation on the left and a valley falling away to

the right wherein you will see nestled the village of **Bleddfa**. In the distance to the far right are the high hills around Knighton.

⑥ Continuing down this track for half a mile will bring you to the edge of the plantation and a gate through which lies an area of rough pasture. The track you need lies in front of the fence that is visible in the dip down to your right. The footpath turns fractionally right and descends through the

---

The Radnor Dragon
The church at Llanfihangel Cascob, on a hillside overlooking a brook, is dedicated, like so many others throughout the land with such a vantage-point, to St Michael (or 'Mihangel' in Welsh) and all his Angels. Unusually though, this church is just one of four in the area all of which are connected to this patron saint of warriors and the suffering: those at Llanfihangel Cefnllys, Llanfihangel Rhydithon and Llanfihangel Nant Melan being the others. The legend tells how the very last of the great Welsh dragons lies sleeping somewhere beneath the mountains of the Radnor Forest and the churches were built as a kind of safety net to contain it. If any one of them is destroyed, then the worm will awaken once more and cause havoc amongst the people of the surrounding country.

Cascob Church

field to join the path. If you have a map you will notice a footpath that rises from the track up over a small hill, **Storling Bank**, to rejoin the track further down this small valley. However, considering the broken stile in the fence and the lack of any sign or discernible path, descending right, down the track itself, seems the most practical option.

⑦ Two-thirds of a mile later you will arrive through a gate that leads to the fore of **Nant-y-corddi Farm**. Your route lies in the dip down to your right, where a track crosses a small brook to continue on between two groups of trees. Just beyond the trees you will find the old drovers' road; follow this to the right and up through a gate onto another banked track.

Continue along the three-quarters of a mile it takes to ascend to the top of the hill that lies ahead.

Initially it rises through a field, before entering the wood a quarter of a mile later. Here you will encounter a forestry turning-circle on the other side of which the track continues up through a gate, whose post has a yellow footpath arrow and a sign: 'Radnor Forest Valleys Association'.

On your way up, the track crosses two forestry roads. One hundred yards after the second of these you arrive at the hilltop and come to the large, red corrugated barn of **Woodgate Farm**. A gate here leads out of the woodland onto a small lane. Descending this for one hundred yards will bring you to a T-junction at which point, bearing left for three-quarters of a mile, you will be back down at your start point.

Walk 13
Knill

Distance: 14 miles
Map: OS Explorer 201

① You can park in the churchyard. Turn left out of Knill churchyard onto the lane that leads back to the main road, and twenty yards on you will find a footpath sign on your left opposite a farmyard. Take this path for one hundred and fifty yards as it ascends a small field towards a gate in a fence.

Beyond this the path continues for three hundred yards, past a large pond on the right and through the gap in the trees ahead of you.

At this point it takes a sharp left along a garden hedge for one hundred and fifty yards towards a stream where you cross over a small wooden bridge into a field. Here the path takes a sharp right to follow the edge of the field and straight on through two more for three-quarters of a mile, until it reaches

Ascending Rushock Hill along King Offa's dyke

the field's edge at **Lower Harpton Farm** next to the **B4362**. A stile here takes you on to a drive adjacent to the barns that face you. You are now on the **Offa's Dyke** Path (ODP), the signposts for which you will be following for the next couple of miles.

2 Turning left up the drive towards the base of **Herrock Hill**, the path soon leaves it to cross for two hundred yards over a small field through two wooden gates to a slighter higher, adjacent track. This curves around the hill past a couple of cottages to ascend a dingle that will eventually bring you, ¾ of a mile further on, high up on the other side of Herrock Hill to an ODP signpost and a large information board entitled 'Herrock Hill Common'.

At this point follow the arrowed path that ascends up to the gate/stile that nestles in the woodland up to your left. Continuing on for another fifty yards will bring you, past the plantation on your left, to another stile beyond where the top of **Rushock Hill** can be seen to level off.

3 The path now follows one of the best preserved sections of the dyke, possibly second only to that found on Llanfair Hill north of Knighton (see **Walk 8**). As you continue, the panorama that opens out here is equally captivating. On the horizon straight ahead are the Clee Hills above Ludlow and then, as you swing clockwise around, you will see the Clent Hills, the Malverns, Bromsgrove Downs, the Black Hill, Hay Bluff, Brecon Beacons and the hills of Radnor Forest. At the very top, the path bends to the right as it passes a small group of firs. A quarter of a mile and two stiles later, you will reach another large tri-arrowed signpost.

4 One arrow points in the direction that you have just come – 'Lower Harpton 1½ m' and another points right to 'Kington 2m', the route the ODP now takes. You, though, need the one pointing straight on: 'To The Mortimer Trail 1/3 mile'. Climbing over the adjacent stile, you will see in the distance your destination: the woodland by the fields on the edge of **Little Brampton Scar**.

The immediate path takes you, for a third of a mile, diagonally across a large field that gradually descends the northern flank of the hill. It's not too well marked, but following the correct direction will take you to the left of a fence and its corner, and down towards the trees in the elbow of the field where they meet a large hedge descending from the right. Along this the **Mortimer Trail** path (MTP) runs. As you approach this corner you will see a gap in which there is an old five-bar gate and the stile that you need to cross. You will be following the well-signed MTP for the next couple of miles.

Initially it takes you along the left-hand edge of a bracken-filled clearing, with a planting of young beech trees to your left. One hundred yards further on, you will reach the wooded edge. At this point the route turns right and follows the MTP through the woodland and along the edge of Little Brampton Scar, with the valley falling away to your left.

(*Alternatives: A signpost another hundred yards further on indicates a footpath that would shorten the walk, which descends from here down through the woods to Knill.*

A shortening descent is also possible a mile further on at SO312609, this time with two different, though fairly steep, footpath options: the first would take you down to Little Brampton Farm, and the second, fifty yards further on, would take you down to Nash, with the result that a slightly longer return journey would be needed to get back to Knill – see below for details.)

This walk, though, carries on along the aptly named 'Green Lane' for ¾ of a mile to **Green Lane Farm** (SO323614), which sits at the end of the escarpment.

Here the MTP veers right, just past a large, open barn to make its long descent east down into Titley.

⑤ At this point, as you face the farm, you will notice another old green lane joining it from the left and rising up through a gate from Rodd Hurst and Presteigne. However, the path you need is sign-posted fifty yards back on the left-hand side, just before you reach the barn.

Over the stile the path directs you diagonally left for one hundred and fifty yards across the field, around the garden for two hundred yards, then through a steel gate beyond which it straightens up. Three hundred yards later you come to a road and the old **Turnpike Cottage** at the hamlet of **Nash**.

⑥ Turning left onto the lane, after one hundred yards you will see a signpost pointing up a hedged green lane off the road to the left. Follow this for two thirds of a mile until it brings you past the wooden barns of **Little Brampton Farm**.

⑦ With the farmhouse on your left you will find yourself facing a hedge and a T-junction of tracks. To the left a hedged track snakes up to Little Brampton Scar along which you have just walked

Burnt House on Little Brampton Scar

The ford at Knill

(or may even have descended, if you took one of the 'shortening' options mentioned previously). To the right the green lane continues and this is the direction you need to take as it will bring you, two-thirds of a mile later, back to your starting-point.

As you approach Knill the path descends by a gate and then, keeping to the right, through a wooded dingle in which is secreted a delightful ford adjacent to two brick-work cottages. The footpath sign take you over the narrow Knill Bridge and hence back into the village a quarter of a mile further on. Looking back across the ford, you will notice another track lying between the cottages, the 'shortening' one previously mentioned, which meets the MTP you walked earlier, above the wooded scar to which it rises.

Gladestry

Walk 14
Hergest Ridge

Distance: 5½ miles
Map: Explorer OS 201

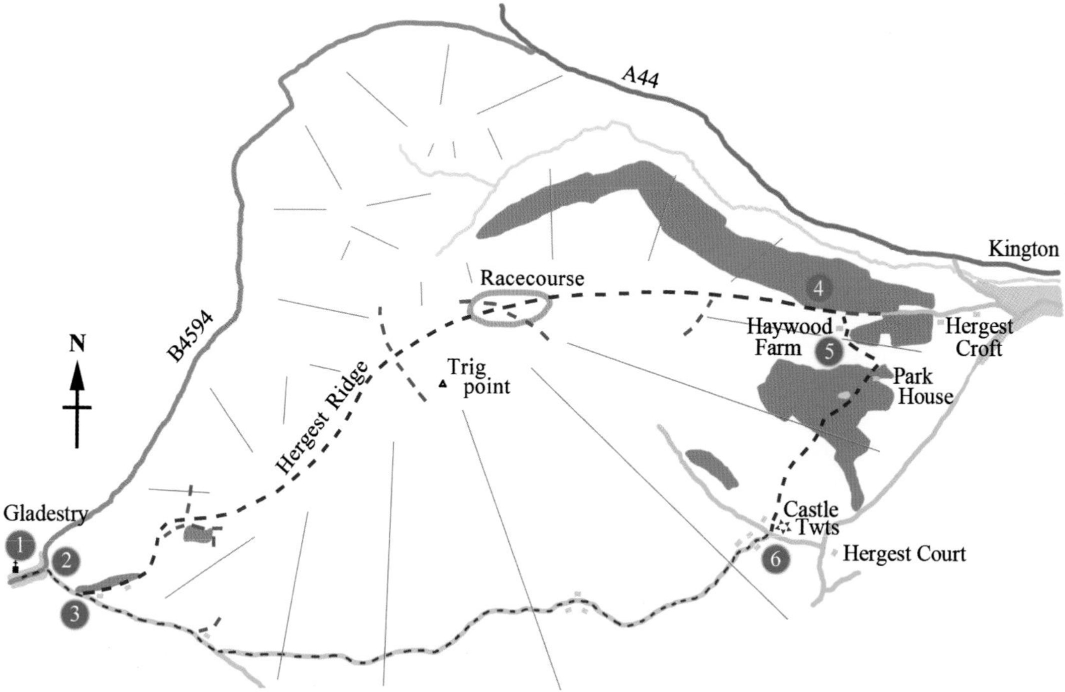

1 With the gates to Gladestry churchyard at your back, head left for two hundred yards down through the village, past the pub and towards the large hill (Yewtree Bank) that rises in front of you.

2 Arriving at a T-junction, follow the road to the right (signed 'Huntington').

3 Another two hundred yards on, there is a signpost for the Offa's Dyke Path (ODP) pointing up the narrow lane that diverts up the hillside to your left. Take this, following the well-signed ODP for the next two miles as it rises over **Hergest Ridge** into **Kington**. Initially the path rises up this lane until, just past the white cottage

N

A44

B4594

Hergest Ridge

Racecourse

Trig point

Kington

Haywood Farm

Hergest Croft

Park House

Castle Twts

Hergest Court

Gladestry

The Whetstone on Hergest Ridge

Hergest Ridge

Pronounced 'hargest' (with a hard 'g'), this area of upland arches up to 1,397 feet above sea level at its trig-point. Near the top, a Victorian racecourse can still be traced both on Ordnance Survey maps and on the ground. It was popular county-wide from 1825 right into the 1880s and replaced one on nearby Bradnor Hill, which now boasts the highest golf course in England, at 1,100ft above sea level.

Looking east from the Whetstone, a large glacial deposit of metamorphic origin atop the northern edge of the ridge, there is no higher ground between here and the Urals of Russia. As the name suggests the boulder itself may have been used for sharpening metal implements or, as Alfred Watkins prefers, it denotes a place where in ancient times trading in such stones or 'slips' used to take place. The 'Black Dog of Hergest' reputedly haunts the ridge, and a sighting of its menacing features is said to presage an imminent death. It would be hard to consider it a mere coincidence that Conan Doyle stayed at the nearby Hergest Hall shortly before he wrote about the infamous hound of the Baskervilles. In more recent times the ridge also proved an inspiration for the composer Mike Oldfield, who lived for a time on Bradnor Hill during the 1970s, and wrote and recorded two successful albums during this time – *Hergest Ridge* and *Ommadawn*.

on the left, it passes through a gate. Continuing to gradually ascend, a quarter of a mile further on the track leaves the hedged lane and rises up onto open countryside.

The wide drove tracks and ODP signposts are easy to follow as you continue for a mile straight up over the hill's brow. Here the trig point, signifying the very top, is visible to your right and all around is an ever-widening panorama. Another half a mile and as you begin the gradual descent of the northern slope of the common you will pass through an area that was once used as a race course.

A mile later the track reaches a treeline that marks the common's edge. Here you will find a steel gate and a stile that you will need to cross and, just beyond, a large information board entitled 'Hergest Ridge Common'.

(*Alternative: A little further down the lane you will pass a 'Welcome to Kington' sign and you may very well wish to make a detour into the town, passing **Hergest Croft Gardens** (which has a tea shop) and St. Mary's church.*)

4 Our walk follows the path that is signed three hundred yards beyond the information point, along the track that descends to your right. After two hundred yards, this brings you into the yard of **Haywood Farm** through which you pass, keeping a group of large pines that stand in the ornamental grounds of Hergest Croft Gardens to your left. Follow the track to the left and downhill for three hundred and fifty yards to a short section of wall.

5 Here the track meets another one coming from the right. At this point, follow the footpath sign that points along this track accompanied by another at ground level for 'Park Wood 13': an ornamental woodland through which the signed footpath passes for the next half a mile. Enter this via a small wooden gate adjacent to a cattle grid.

The path continues to rise up through the woodland, past **Park House** to the left and an ornamental pond on the right, until it reaches the edge of the woodland, where a stile sits in the hedge to the left of another ground-level sign: 'Log Cabin 17'. Passing through this stile, the path crosses the field diagonally right for one hundred and fifty yards, to meet another stile nestled in a hedge. Through this, the path continues for the next quarter of a mile along the top edge of this field, through two more stiles that sit either side of two narrow strip-fields separated by an adjoining hedge, before

A view from Hergest Ridge

Castle Twts motte and bailey, Lower Hergest

6 In the far corner a stile brings you onto a lane by the hamlet of Lower Hergest. Follow the lane straight ahead, through Upper Hergest and three miles back to Gladestry village, skirting the southern flank of Hergest Ridge along which you walked earlier.

continuing a gradual descent along the top edge of the next field.

Just beyond this field you will clearly see in the foreground the distinctive mound of a motte and bailey (**Castle Twts**), around whose right-hand flank the path will take you. This is reached through the stile at the far edge of the final field that you will cross on this walk, up through a small dingle via a tiny one-plank bridge. This brings you above an old track into the small field containing the motte and bailey.

Pine trees on Merbach Hill

Walk 15
Merbach Hill, Bredwardine

Distance: 5 miles
Map: OS Explorer 201

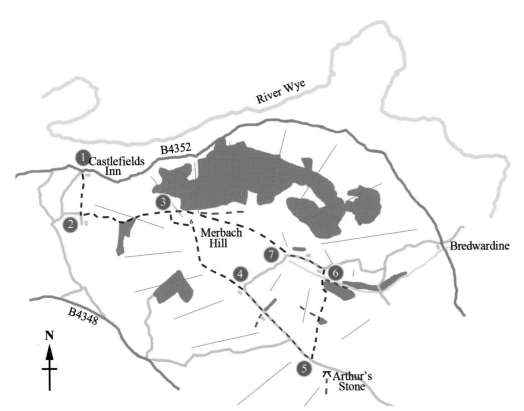

This walk begins just before the **Castlefields Inn** on the **B4352** road from Hay to Bredwardine. Here you will find a minor road signed to 'Middlewood' and alongside it a green lane (SO291452) along which an old drovers' road (mentioned by Shirley Toulson) once ascended over Merbach Hill, thus avoiding the tollgate further along the road. It is also the route followed by the well-signed 'Wye Valley Walk' (WVW). There is a useful small layby two hundred yards further down the road on the right-hand side.

Overlooking the Wye west of Merbach Hill

❶ Facing the lane you will notice a road sign, 'Merbach', and another informing drivers that this is 'Unsuitable for motors', an understatement if ever there was one. One hundred yards further on, though, the grass gives way to a harder surface more suitable for vehicles, before merging with a tarmacked lane that emerges from the right a quarter of a mile further on.

❷ Continue straight on for another fifty yards and you will find another 'Merbach' road sign pointing up to the left, alongside a signpost for the WVW. The latter signs you continue to follow up this lane as it ascends the hill into the woodland above. Where it becomes narrower, you will encounter a large information board: 'Merbach Hill Common'.

❸ Continuing to ascend another quarter of a mile through the trees into an open area of bracken, you will eventually come to a signpost on the far side. At this point, leave the WVW to turn right along a smaller footpath in the direction of the yellow arrow. This follows the hill around to the right through the bracken and past a red post, before continuing a fairly steep ascent of three hundred yards up towards the summit; you will see a trig point emerging to your left. The panorama here is well worth a pause and includes the Black Mountains and Hay Bluff behind you, and to the far left Hergest Ridge and the hills around Kington.

Straight ahead you will notice how two hundred yards away the path descends slightly to a fence in which sits a small wooden gate, next to another large information board. Go through the gate and continue for half a mile over a large expanse of grazed common, past the small group of trees on the horizon, before descending right towards the hedged corner of the common.

❹ Here a gate leads onto the bend of a road (SO309440). A large signpost directs you straight on if you want to follow the 'Herefordshire Trail' along the drovers' road known as 'Arthur's Stone Lane', and this is indeed the direction in which our walk continues.

(Alternative: A short-cut is possible here that would save you one and a half miles of walking, by simply turning left along the road instead of straight on. A third of a mile later you reach the next bend where you need to turn left along the green lane route described below in section 7.)

5 If you choose to do the full walk, after two thirds of a mile of walking along Arthur's Stone Lane, you will find a bridleway signposted to the left, through a pair of gates which also exhibit a sign for the 'British Horse Society / Long Distance Route'. You need to take this bridle-way, but perhaps not before a slight detour of two hundred yards further along the road to **Arthur's Stone** burial chamber.

The bridleway follows a track along a hedge towards another gate on the other side of which on the crest of the hill there is a group of old firs. The path takes you diagonally left of them towards a large hedge which it then runs alongside down towards a plantation. Before you reach it, though, cross a stile through the small hedge running across the field. On the other side, continue following the arrow that directs you to head diagonally left down towards the corner of the plantation where it meets a large hedge. Pass through this towards another hedge fifty yards away, within which a stile and planked bridge take you over a brook to a path that runs alongside the picket fence of a small cottage.

6 After another fifty yards you will find yourself on a road; turn left for a quarter mile of gradual ascent.

7 Where the road bends sharply to the left (SO314444), you will notice the hedged green lane mentioned above, along which another bridleway is signed. Follow this as it makes its gradual ascent back up towards the top of Merbach Hill. After a third of a mile the bridleway passes through a wooden gate onto the common; but you need to follow the path straight ahead, always keeping to the right, as it continues for another quarter of a mile through a small group of trees and open areas of bracken until, approaching the brow of the hill, it bears downhill to the right.

Arthur's Stone

A Neolithic chambered burial tomb, or dolmen, constructed around 5,000 years ago, it consists of nine uprights supporting a huge capstone, 25 tonnes in weight. The whole would have originally been covered by an earthen mound some 25 metres in length and accessed from the side via its right-angled passage. It has never been excavated, but it is likely to have once contained the remains of several ancients alongside their knapped flints, arrowheads and pottery. The isolated 'Quoit Stone' that lies to the south bears indentations said to have been impressed by the elbows and knees of King Arthur himself whilst kneeling at prayer.

Stone dolmen, Merbach Hill

Two hundred yards later it meets the WVW in a clearing where, if you happen to be here in late June, you will find a community of spotted orchids. Turning left here will bring you back, after a quarter of a mile, to the signpost where you previously headed to the right. Continue straight on down the WVW to arrive back at your starting-point in the valley below.

The Rhydspence Inn

Four miles to the west across the river Wye, the Rhydspence Inn has droving connections right down to the grass roots of its name, 'rhyd' referring to 'river crossing' and 'pence' to the cost of the pasture to which animals were put. However, the original building of 1380 is said to predate even the droving trade, having been a stopping point for medieval pilgrims en route from Abbeycwmhir to Hereford Cathedral. The Vaughan family of Hergest are thought to have built it, and the most infamous of them – Black Vaughan – is said to ride his ghostly charger down the nave of Kington Church to this day. The inn is of a design known as a 'Hall House': two-storey, with a large barn area opening out at one end and a centrally placed fire. Over time conversions saw the upper storey extended throughout and the thatched roof changed to one of stone tiles. Following the dissolution of the monasteries the form and usage of the inn gradually changed so as to accommodate the increasing number of drovers who followed the 'Black Ox trail' out of Wales into England towards their next overnight stop at Hereford. In fact the border follows the stream that runs through the garden, the inn being situated on the English bank. There was also a smithy here, the Rhydspence having been an important shoeing station for animals prior to their journey along the harder English roads. And the inn had a cider press (last used in 1956 and still visible today) to slake the drovers' thirst, cider having become a popular [...] ring the 18th century. A private dwelling on the Welsh side is said once to have been another inn.

Walk 16
Bromyard Downs

Distance: 4 miles
Map: OS Explorer 202

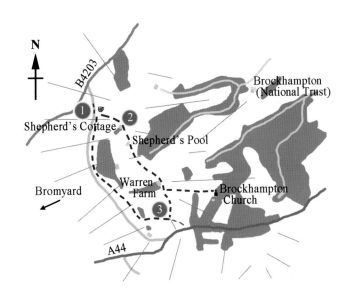

❶ From the designated car-park situated on the downs (at SO670558), turn right along the unfenced road along which you will have just driven. (This was probably part of an important north-south thoroughfare in its own right, as suggested by the presence of the turnpike cottage (at SO673548) three-quarters of a mile to the south.) This direction will take you to the front of the adjacent Royal Oak, an inn well known for its droving connections.

Just past the inn, start walking uphill onto the open grassland of the downs. Head diagonally to the right for a third of a mile up towards the trees and the corner of the field, where you will find a gate (at SO674556). Through this, hidden away in a small copse, is **Shepherd's Cottage**, an old abandoned residence and one no doubt well known to the drovers, who perhaps even stayed here themselves.

❷ Beyond the cottage the concessionary footpath joins a wide track that leads past **Shepherds Pool** for half a mile to **Warren Farm**, another establishment whose pines, size and antiquity might suggest a droving connection. From here the route carries straight on, although if you have time and energy to spare, you might care to drop down the signed footpath to the left (at SO678549) to visit **Brockhampton Church**.

3 A third of a mile later (at SO678545) you will reach a footpath signposted to your right. Here the original drove route would have carried on downhill to the A44 and thence east to Worcester or south-east to Malvern. However, you need to take this path, which ascends by the hedge for three hundred yards up to the escarpment of the downs. Here you will gain great views to the west, over Bromyard town and beyond into Herefordshire and Wales.

Now you start the mile-long return journey back to the car-park, by initially heading right along the edge of the wood. This well-marked path goes via a copse of Scots pines (SO673549) and then through Warren Wood. Detours can be made at any point from this path, down over the grassland to the road visible below, maybe to visit the aforementioned turnpike cottage or even into Bromyard itself.

The Bromyard Races
As in Kington and Knighton, the townsfolk of Bromyard used a suitable area of nearby high ground (the 'downs') to establish a racecourse. This one was built in 1815 as a means of providing gainful employment for the 'Bromyard Volunteers', the large number of returning soldiers who found themselves unemployed during the economic slump that followed the Napoleonic wars. At the height of the racecourse's popularity in 1884 an estimated crowd of 7,000 came from as far afield as Birmingham, Worcester and Hereford, to enjoy five races – one on the flat, four over fences. The finish line was at a point above the Royal Oak Inn, just below the crest of the hill, where a grandstand was situated. From here race-goers could enjoy seeing horses careering down the track that headed left below Shepherd's Cottage, to cross the downs road near to the Old Bowling Green below which most of the jumps were situated. Apparently the water jumps were fed by their own springs, while the discerning Victorian punter would have had six 'watering holes' in the immediate vicinity to choose from for their own liquid refreshment and victuals, the Royal Oak being the only one that survives to this day.

Looking south over the Bromyard Downs towards the Malverns

Across Wales and the Middle Marches from Gospel Pass

Further reading

Bonser, K.J. – *The Drovers*, Macmillan, 1970

Bunting, Madeleine – *The Plot*, Granta, 2009

Hughes, P.G. – *Wales and the Drovers*, Golden Grove, 1988 (originally published 1943)

Hughes, T.J. – *Wales's Best One Hundred Churches*, Seren, 2006

Hurley, Heather – *The Old Roads of South Herefordshire: Trackway to Turnpike*, Fineleaf, 2007 (2nd revised edition)

Hurley, Heather – *The Green Lanes of Herefordshire*, Fineleaf, 2010

Macfarlane, Hamish – *The Old Ways*, Hamish Hamilton, 2012

Moore-Colyer, Richard – *Roads and Trackways of Wales*, Moorland, 1984

Moore-Colyer, Richard – *The Welsh Cattle Drovers*, Landmark, 2002 (originally published 1976)

Moore-Colyer, Richard – *Genuki: Welsh Cattle Drovers in the Nineteenth Century*, National Library of Wales Journal, 1972-75

Toulson, Shirley and Godwin, Fay – *The Drovers' Roads of Wales*, Wildwood House, 1977

Toulson, Shirley – *The Drovers*, Shire Books, 2005

Wheeler, Richard – *The Medieval Church Screens of the Southern Marches*, Logaston Press, 2006

Herefordshire Lore – *In Our Age*, Summer 2007 Issue 5, p2

Index